Praise for CREATE

I have long been a fan of Bethany's work, and this book has me hooked again. It really illuminates the idea that great teaching is not about the use of technology, but rather how we make use of it to empower learning. It is loaded with great examples, accessible straight from the embedded QR codes. Each of the QR code exemplars shows exactly how we can help kids more effectively share what they've learned through the CREATE process. This book is easy to follow and a must-have for anyone wanting to incorporate technology in really interesting and meaningful ways.

—**Holly Clark**, speaker, blogger, and author of the Infused Classroom series

CREATE is a fantastic book that will show you how to amplify student voices and tap into the four Cs in your classroom. In this easy-to-read guide, Bethany shares ready-made templates and lesson ideas that any teacher can use.

—**Kasey Bell**, author, speaker, blogger, and podcaster, ShakeUpLearning.com

Bethany Petty uses her teaching experience to craft a book that sets up the next generation of innovators for success. She goes deep on how to foster modern writing opportunities and develop the citizen-ready skills of media creation that solve real-world problems. Petty finishes what she starts by guiding teachers through ways to assess and evaluate these authentic work products. Grab this book today.

—**Dr. Robert Dillon**, educator, author, learner

Creating is an imperative step in learning, allowing students to show what they know in authentic ways, and bringing purpose to classroom lessons. CREATE is sure to inspire and support teachers of all levels with new ideas, practical tools, and guidance for how to design lessons that allow all students to demonstrate their learning.

—**Lisa Highfill**, co-creator of *Teachers Give Teachers* and author of *The HyperDoc Handbook*

Struggling to keep students motivated and empowered to create? This book is the solution for YOU! Throughout the pages of *CREATE*, Bethany Petty presents innovative ways to supply students with **C**hoice. I admire how she shares the importance of providing **R**elevance to our current reality. And it doesn't stop there. Creation is most meaningful when done with a purpose, and Bethany provides various ways to have the learners show **E**vidence of their learning and check for understanding using multiple forms of **A**ssessment. The way the book is laid out alleviates the stress of integrating **T**ech in the classroom and ultimately sets the stage for classrooms to erupt with student **E**ngagement. If you want to reinvigorate your teaching delivery and excite your learners to reach new heights, *CREATE* is the book for you!

—**Tara M. Martin**, educator, author, Director of PR and communication at DBC, Inc.

CREATE

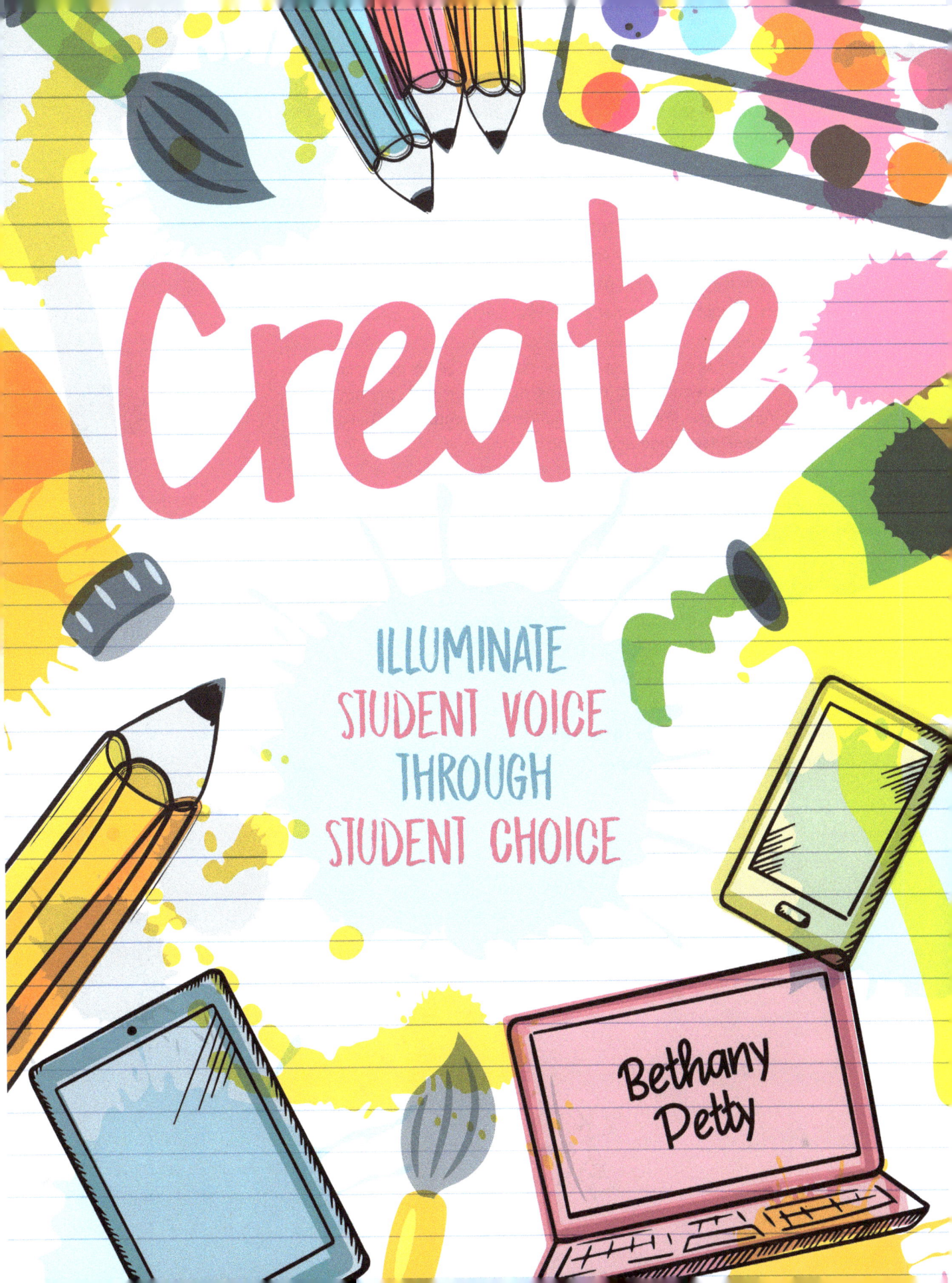

CREATE: Illuminate Student Voice through Student Choice
© 2020 Bethany J. Petty

All rights reserved. No part of this publication may be reproduced in any form or by any electronic or mechanical means, including information storage and retrieval systems, without permission in writing by the publisher, except by a reviewer, who may quote brief passages in a review. For information regarding permission, contact the publisher at books@daveburgessconsulting.com.

> This book is available at special discounts when purchased in quantity for educational purposes or as premiums, promotions, or fundraisers. For inquiries and details, contact the publisher at books@daveburgessconsulting.com.

Published by Dave Burgess Consulting, Inc.
San Diego, CA
DaveBurgessConsulting.com

Library of Congress Control Number: 2020939120
Paperback ISBN: 978-1-951600-28-0
Ebook ISBN: 978-1-951600-29-7

Cover and interior design by Liz Schreiter
Author Photo by Brittany Juliette

In loving memory of James Walter Wilson Jr.

For Hanna and Molly

I am incredibly proud of you and so thankful to be your mommy.
Remember the message of Psalm 46:5.

For Issac

Thank you for your continuous love, support, and encouragement.

For Mom and Dad

Thank you for raising me to believe I can do anything.

CONTENTS

Introduction: CREATE in the Classroom 1
- Tools for Making Creativity Happen 1
- There's a Word for It 1
- Putting CREATE into Action 3

1: Creating with Social Media 5
- No Platform Required 5
- Facebook/Fakebook Techniques 6
- Instagram 8
- Twitter 10
- Snapchat 12
- It's All about Choice 14

2: Creating Video and Audio Products 16
- Show What You Know 16
- Easing Anxiety 17
- Video Tutorials 17
- Easy Video Options 18
- CREATE Video Activities 19
- Creating through Podcasts 20
- CREATE Podcast Activities 22
- Learn, Create, Present, Repeat 22

3: Creating through Writing 24
- Getting the Words down Is Key 24
- Blogging for Teachers and Students 24
- Blogging Choices 25
- Use Those Writing Skills 26
- Writing with E-books 27
- E-book Writing Choices 27
- A Classroom of Authors 27
- Writing through Text Messaging 29
- Writing Web Pages and Creating Websites 31
- Using Web Pages to Develop Writing Skills 31

4: Creating with Games 34
- Playing Games Takes Brains 34
- Low-Tech/No-Tech Games... 37
- Creating Games to Demonstrate Learning 39

5: Creating with Visual Aids 41
- Don't Forget Low-Tech—A Pencil and Paper Are Options, Too.......... 41
- Using BOARD Time to Demonstrate Learning 41
- Creating Visual Aids to Demonstrate Learning 43
- Say It in Pictures 48

6: Evaluating Creations 50
- The Challenge of Differentiation.................................... 50
- A Great New Tool 52
- Frequent Self-Assessment of Learning 54

7: Sharing Creations 56
- An Audience beyond the Classroom............................... 56
- Audience Appreciation... 58

Conclusion: It's Time To CREATE! 61
Appendix: Tech Tool Index 62
Acknowledgments 65
About the Author 67
More from Dave Burgess Consulting, Inc. 69

Introduction: CREATE in the Classroom

As every teacher knows, dynamic things happen in a creative classroom. When we're not limited to handing out a single repetitive assignment to thirty students and when students have a choice in how best to demonstrate what they're learning—stand back and watch the fireworks.

TOOLS FOR MAKING CREATIVITY HAPPEN

Today, creativity in the classroom can, but doesn't have to be, linked with technology. Every subject area and every career, from the sciences to business to education and the arts, now relies on a sound fluency in tech skills. Fortunately, learning and teaching these techniques is exciting, and using the wealth of internet tools specifically designed for teachers in the classroom makes sharing, experimenting, creating, and learning a dynamic experience.

That's what CREATE is all about. In the following chapters we'll explore the many tools available: how to access them and how to use them, with examples of creative projects for each. My area happens to be high school social studies, but teachers of all subjects and all age groups can apply these tools and strategies to the needs of their own classrooms.

THERE'S A WORD FOR IT

To illustrate the aims of this book and the goals of a creative classroom, I created a handy acronym that will appear as a reminder throughout the chapters:

CHOICE, RELEVANCE, EVIDENCE, ASSESSMENT, TECH, ENGAGEMENT = CREATE

CHOICE

Through meaningful tech integration in the classroom, teachers can offer their students more **choices** for demonstrating what they've learned. Do they like to write essays? Let them go for it. Would they prefer to create a visual presentation using a sketchnote, mind map, or another tool? Great. Do they

want to try their hand at creating a game to demonstrate their grasp of a subject? How about a tweet? All good. Students take more ownership and pride in a project when their **choice** is taken into account. If you think about it, we all take more pride in our work when we have an option on how we share the information.

RELEVANCE

Before I present a seminar or a workshop for teachers, I always ask my students for their thoughts on topics I should bring up and discuss with my audience. Most of their suggestions are usually about the way we gamify our classroom, but one student's comment stopped me in my tracks when I asked what I should tell a teacher who is totally against using technology in the classroom. "Technology is just more **relevant** for us," the student said, "because this is what we know, and we use it every day." Absolutely. By providing students with choice in how they complete classroom activities and encouraging them to learn and experiment with a range of tech skills, we increase the **relevance** of their assignments because they discover how best to translate their ideas, and they become more invested in the product they create.

EVIDENCE

As teachers, we focus on what our students are learning in our classrooms. We frequently assess their work as we proceed through the study units, looking for **evidence** that they comprehend and know how to use the material we've covered. When students create their own representations of what they've learned, teachers are better able—with the support of rubrics tied to standards—to assess that **evidence**.

ASSESSMENT

By using frequent evaluation, students and teachers can **assess** learning progress in relation to the relevant targets and standards. Throughout this book, we will be looking at different tools and strategies for creating effective rubrics that are tied to learning standards. In addition, we'll **assess** how we as teachers can encourage our students to evaluate their own learning, so they can see for themselves where they need help or clarification in their understanding of content.

TECH

It's important to remember (and sometimes easy to forget in our twenty-first-century classrooms) that, while lessons and activities can be "high-**tech**," they can also be "no-**tech**." Increased access to technology in classrooms all over the world clearly provides students and teachers with amazing opportunities, but technology is only one tool for the classroom; it's not a requirement for learning. Some students may learn more effectively by sketching out their ideas using paper and pencil, rather than initiating ideas as infographics on their Chromebooks. This is perfectly fine. It all comes back to choice.

ENGAGEMENT

By providing students with choices in how they demonstrate what they are learning, we are encouraging them to **engage** in our classroom environment. Every one of us takes more pride and ownership in a product when we have a choice in how we approach it—because then it's *ours*. Our students may choose to **engage** by creating a blog or a simulated Twitter profile, rather than writing an essay to demonstrate their understanding. In doing so, they'll connect more fully to their subject because their choice helped them think about the subject creatively.

> The technology at our disposal should never become so important that its use overshadows the content we are teaching or our recognition of the way each student learns best. It's not about the tech, it's how you use it!

PUTTING CREATE INTO ACTION

Throughout this book, we'll look at a variety of strategies, tools, and templates that you can use tomorrow in your classroom to encourage your students to CREATE, including:

- creating with social media
- creating through writing
- creating with visual aids
- creating with games
- creating through video and audio products

We'll also discuss how teachers can create evaluation tools that provide effective and timely feedback for our students' creations, and we'll look at ways to help our students create and share work with an authentic audience (one that feels relevant and important to our students), which will encourage them to feel a greater sense of pride and ownership in their work.

What do you say?
Are you ready to create?
Let's get to it!

1
Creating with Social Media

NO PLATFORM REQUIRED

Our students today have never known a time when there was no social media. For them, instantly sharing pictures, videos, messages, and comments seems completely natural. As teachers, we can use this to our advantage by creating fun, engaging, and effective learning opportunities using the social media tools available online that have been developed especially for the classroom.

> **You Don't Need a Social Media Account to Learn Social Media Techniques**
>
> Using social media platforms like Facebook, Instagram, Twitter, and Snapchat, regardless of the positive potential they may bring to motivating students, may simply not work in the classroom. Parents will want to choose when their children are old enough have social media accounts and which platforms they will allow. School districts may have specific policies that prevent the use of social media in the classroom, while teachers may not feel comfortable using these tools in their classrooms and students may simply be too young. However, teachers can leverage the popularity and enticing pull of social media tools without even creating an account. Every technique in this chapter uses student-friendly digital classroom tools that mimic actual social media tools.

 Create

FACEBOOK/FAKEBOOK TECHNIQUES

Why offer Facebook templates as an assignment for your students? When students are able to demonstrate what they've learned using a familiar medium that allows them to apply course concepts in a fun way, the end product can give us an insightful glimpse into how they've grasped the subject.

FACEBOOK/FAKEBOOK TEMPLATES

CLASSTOOLS

Accessing the tool
- Teachers can access "Fakebook" templates and many other useful resources at classtools.net.

Student use
- Students click on the Fakebook image to access the template, and then add pictures, cover images, and text to create their page. Students save their work through ClassTools and can return to it later.

Sharing and submitting work
- Students can submit their Fakebook pages through Google Classroom. After teachers create an assignment in Classroom, students add their work through the "add" link feature in the assignment.

GOOGLE SLIDES

Accessing the tool
- Teachers can create a Facebook template using Google Slides or Google Drawings (see image).

Student use
- Students can easily edit templates created with Google Slides or Google Drawings by adding images, videos, "friends," events, groups, and more. Teachers assign these templates through Google Classroom and can easily create a copy for each student.

Sharing and submitting work
- When teachers assign a Facebook template using Google Classroom, students can make edits to their copy before submitting it.

Use Facebook templates in your classroom to:

- **Demonstrate knowledge of a historical event.** How would America's founders like George Washington and Benjamin Franklin have felt about the Civil War if they had been alive to witness it? Create a Facebook profile (as illustrated) for a historical character based on what students have learned about him or her can encourage students to think critically about an event from a different perspective.
- **Share the perspective of a character from a book.** What would Jem and Scout from *To Kill a Mockingbird* include in their Facebook profiles? Who would they be friends with? What pages would they like? What images or posts would they like or share? Why?
- **Share opinions about a scientific discovery.** Students can imagine that they lived during the time of a scientific achievement, such as Marie Curie's discovery of radium. What was important about the discovery at the time? How would it be used? What questions would they have for Marie?

Use Facebook templates in your classroom in a variety of ways to encourage students to think critically, apply their knowledge, and have fun doing so!

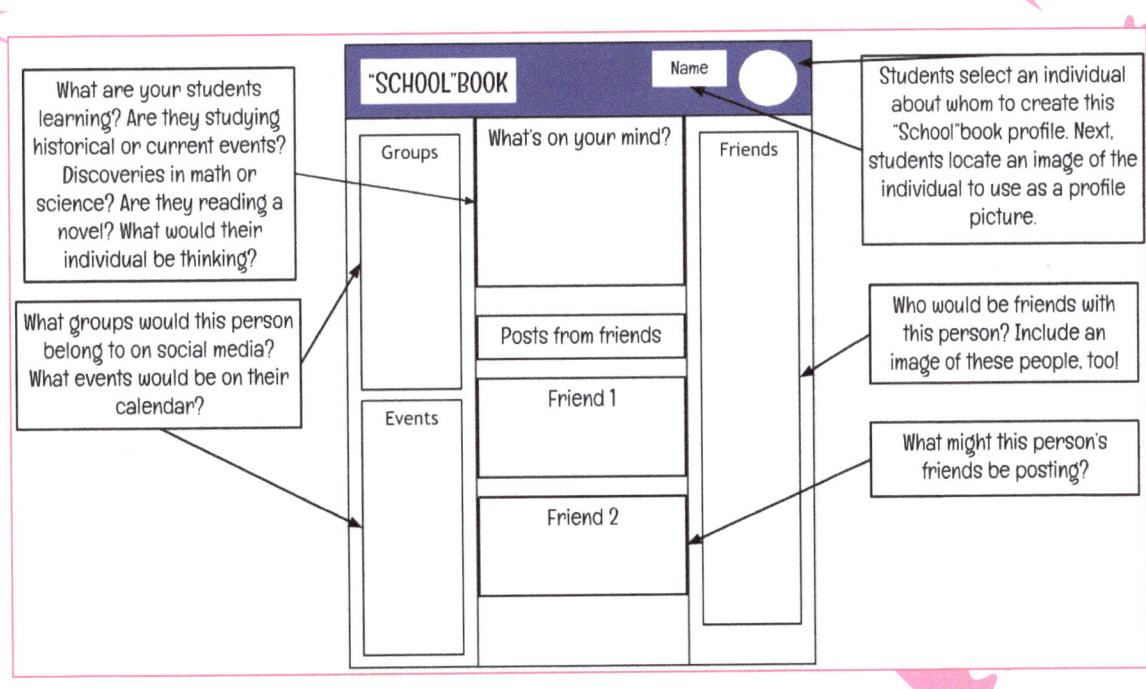

 *Create*

INSTAGRAM

Capitalize on the popularity of Instagram in your classroom by offering students the opportunity to share what they've learned through an Instagram post. Creating Instagram-like posts about an event, discovery, concept, or contribution will help students think critically about the topic by imagining how an individual who experienced the event might have felt as it happened.

INSTAGRAM TEMPLATES

GENERATE STATUS

Accessing the tool
- Teachers and students can access Generate Status at generatestatus.com.

Student use
- Students can easily upload images to create a profile picture and Instagram-like post. Generate Status allows users to include a username, post time, number of likes, and a message. Students can then download the image to their device.

Sharing and submitting work
- Teachers can easily create an assignment in Classroom, and students can add their Instagram-like posts through the "add" link feature in the assignment.

GOOGLE SLIDES

Accessing the tool
- Teachers can create a quick Instagram template using Google Slides or Google Drawings (scan QR code).

Student use
- Students can search for and insert images into their post without leaving the Slides template. After identifying the individual they want to highlight in their post, students create a username and a post about an event that the individual experienced. Teachers can set their own character count and/or word requirement for this post and may encourage their students to include relevant hashtags with the post. Students then create a QR code that links to an additional resource about the topic/event/individual.

Sharing and submitting work
- In Classroom, teachers can create an assignment and then choose the "make a copy" option for each student. Students can then edit the file and submit their assignment.

Use Instagram templates in your classroom to:

- **Evaluate the decisions made by world leaders.** What if President Truman had an Instagram page? What would he have shared the day he decided to use nuclear weapons on Japan? How would citizens have responded to his decision?
- **Identify important contributions of famous people.** Sacagawea was the Shoshone woman who assisted Lewis and Clark as an interpreter and guide. If she had access to Instagram during their exploration of the American West, what kinds of pictures would she have posted? Who would she have tagged in her posts to encourage discussions about what they were seeing and the dangers they were facing? What would she have said about the fate of Native Americans?

TWITTER

I wasn't convinced of the benefits of Twitter when it first appeared. I gave it the cold shoulder for a few years before I created an account and jumped into what would become one of the greatest resources for my teaching career.

Think about how often your students, especially those in the middle and upper grades, begin a sentence with a variation of, "I saw something on Twitter today." In my classroom, this conversation happens on a daily basis. Twitter, like Facebook and Instagram, are part of our students' everyday lives. As teachers, we can definitely capitalize on this familiarity in the classroom.

TWITTER TEMPLATES

TWEETGEN

Accessing the tool
- Teachers and students can access TweetGen at tweetgen.com.

Student use
- Students can easily create a tweet that includes the account name, username, verified status, time and date, replies, retweets, likes, hashtags, and of course, the content of the post.

Sharing and submitting work
- Students can submit these Tweet-like posts through Google Classroom. Teachers simply create an assignment on Classroom, and students add their work through the "add" link feature in the assignment. Teachers might also create a class "Twitter" account on a bulletin board or other classroom space to display student work.

GOOGLE SLIDES

Accessing the tool
- Teachers can create a quick Twitter template using Google Slides or Google Drawings (scan QR code).

Student use
- Students can create a Twitter profile that includes a profile image, tweet, followers, following, and trending hashtags.

Sharing and submitting work
- Teachers create an assignment in Classroom and choose the "make a copy" option for each student. Students can then edit the file and easily submit their assignment.

Use Twitter templates in your classroom to:

- **Describe current events.** How would Abraham Lincoln and Martin Luther King Jr. tweet about race relations in the world today?
- **Share a "new invention."** Ask students to think about what new invention the world needs. Then, assign the Google Slides Twitter template and encourage them to create their futuristic profile where they debut their new creation.
- **Encourage others to read a book.** When my daughter Hannah was in second grade, she already enjoyed blogging about the books she liked to read. By "tweeting" about her favorite books, as well, she could recommend them to her friends.

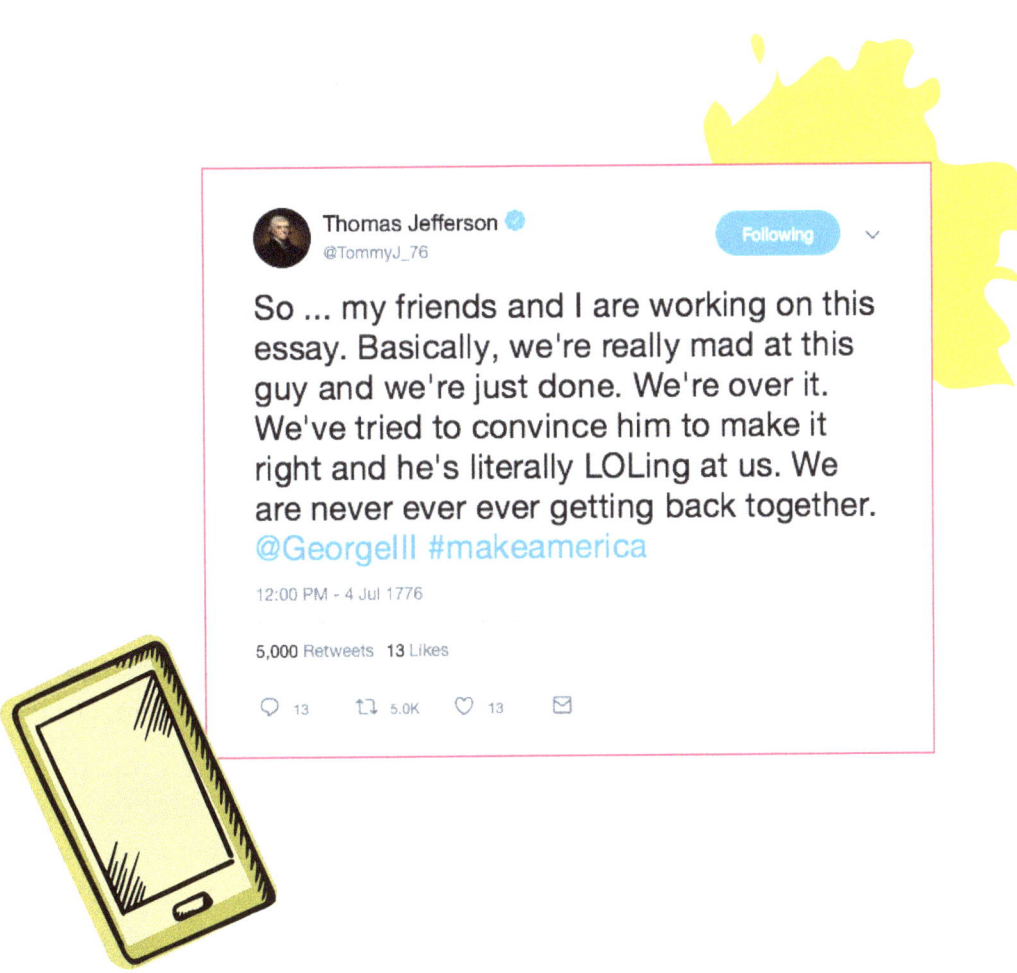

SNAPCHAT

The main characteristic of Snapchat is that the pictures and "stories" shared on it are available only briefly. Among the many fun aspects of the app are the filters, or layovers, that allow users to add color tones and special visual effects to their pictures. Snapchat users can also participate in "chats" with friends.

TWITTER TEMPLATES	
GOOGLE SLIDES (CHAT) 	**Accessing the tool** • Teachers can create a "chat" template similar to Snapchat using Google Drawings or Google Slides (scan QR code). **Student use** • Students can create a fictional conversation between two characters, historical figures, modern leaders, or fellow students. **Sharing and submitting work** • Teachers create an assignment in Classroom and choose the "make a copy" option for each student. Students can then edit the file and submit their assignment.
GOOGLE SLIDES (IMAGE) 	**Accessing the tool** • Teachers can create an image template similar to Snapchat using Google Drawings or Google Slides (scan QR code). **Student use** • Students can create a "snap" that includes an image uploaded from their device or Google Drive, or selected from a web search. They'll then add a comment or reflection about the image from their own perspective or from that of a historical figure, depending on the requirements of the assignment. **Sharing and submitting work** • Teachers can create an assignment in Classroom and choose the "make a copy" option for each student. Students then edit the file and submit their assignment.

How to take advantage of students' familiarity with Snapchat in your classroom:

- **Create "stories" about famous people in history.** Have students document what a famous leader or role model went through as they sought to make a difference in their community.
- **Describe a mathematical or scientific process.** Students create a "Snapchat chat" that describes the Pythagorean Theorem or the scientific method to a real or fictional individual.
- **Reflect upon events from a book.** Students create a chat or image using a Snapchat template to discuss and share an important event from a book. Snapchat templates could provide a neat new twist on a traditional book report.

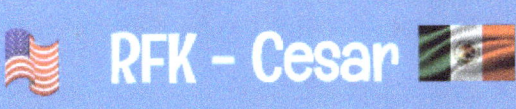

 Create

IT'S ALL ABOUT CHOICE

Although some school districts may not permit the use of social media platforms in the classroom, as teachers we can still take advantage of our students' knowledge of social media skills by introducing templates developed just for us and by encouraging students to create products that demonstrate their understanding of course concepts. We can also use these activities as an opportunity to model appropriate social media conduct and digital citizenship.

> When using social media in the classroom, through activities such as those described in this chapter or by sharing information through Twitter, Facebook, Instagram, and the like, it's vitally important to effectively communicate to our students the importance of maintaining a positive and truthful online presence. While school districts likely have a policy surrounding the use of digital resources for students and staff, teachers can also create an agreement for their students on using social media.

 SCAN THIS CODE FOR A SAMPLE CLASSROOM SOCIAL MEDIA CONTRACT TO USE WITH YOUR STUDENTS!

TRY THIS TOMORROW

Scan the "School"book template and encourage your students to create a social media profile for a fictional character, historical person, or the author of a book. Students can work independently or collaborate with their peers to apply what they have learned—and have fun in the process!

CREATING WITH SOCIAL MEDIA: NOTES

2

Creating Video and Audio Products

SHOW WHAT YOU KNOW

We can all remember things that terrified us in school. For me, it was getting called on in class and having everyone look at me. All I ever wanted was to blend into my desk and quietly observe what was happening in the classroom, absorbing information and waiting to demonstrate my knowledge on the unit test. As a student, I would far rather have had the stomach flu than to have to present in front of my peers.

I like to tell my students this story before they begin a presentation to remind them that not everyone is comfortable standing in front of a class or assembly. Their dear teacher eventually overcame her fear of speaking in front of a room (I've even been known to sing, dance, and rap on my desk), and every one of them can overcome their fears, too.

> **Snap Instead of Clap**
>
> To help ease the angst of presentations, my students and I finger snap instead of clapping after a presentation has been delivered. There are two good reasons to "snap instead of clap." First, it avoids the "slow clap" that many of us endured (or participated in) when we were students. As you read "slow clap," you can probably hear that sound in your head: someone starts off the slow clap and then the others join in. As the presenter, you might brush it off or laugh, but on the inside, you're standing there even more embarrassed than you were when you started your presentation. The other reason we "snap" in our classroom is because it helps to create a laid-back, comfortable learning environment for my students, diffusing the presentation anxiety that so many face.

EASING ANXIETY

Yes, our students need to be able to present information in front of a group: some classroom, district, and national standards even require a class presentation or two. At some point, if not often, in a person's career they will need to deliver a speech or teach a class or chair a meeting, and the earlier they learn to feel comfortable doing so, the happier they will be. If we give our students the opportunity to demonstrate what they have learned by creating a video as a formative or summative assessment of course content, their anxiety about the assignment can decrease, and at the same time provide us with a clear view of what they have learned.

As a teacher, I find that viewing and evaluating video submissions is very much like having a one-on-one conference with each student. I'm able to listen to what they have to say, and then provide them with effective and timely feedback. I can respond with a quick video or provide a written resource that can help clear up any points they might have misunderstood or that might extend their knowledge about subjects that interest them.

> When students create videos to demonstrate understanding, they can verbally present what they have learned from the relaxed atmosphere of their home, the library, or other quiet space, with less anxiety than delivering a traditional presentation.

VIDEO TUTORIALS

Along with my role as a high school social studies teacher, I'm also an adjunct instructor of educational technology and I develop online learning opportunities for educators all over the world. Due to the nature of online learning, it can sometimes be difficult to communicate information and demonstrate understanding through text alone. I find that creating quick video tutorials is a great way for me to help my students navigate our resources.

Although many of my students have never accessed Google Classroom or used Google tools prior to taking my online course, these tools are easily learned. I also encourage my students to screencast any websites or resources they're struggling to use so I can gain a better idea of what assistance they need from me. Whether I design face-to-face, blended, or digital learning experiences for my students, video is a great option for them to use to demonstrate their knowledge.

 Create

EASY VIDEO OPTIONS

While there are many great options for video creation in the classroom, Screencastify, Flipgrid, and the camera app on smartphones are particularly easy-to-use tools. When I evaluate technology for my classroom, I ask myself whether it is easy to use and whether it enhances the lesson or distracts from the purpose. The following tools meet my requirements.

VIDEO CREATION TOOLS	
SCREENCASTIFY 	**Access the tool** • Students and teachers can access Screencastify at screencastify.com and can easily add the extension to their Chrome browser. **Student use** • When students (and teachers) set up Screencastify, they'll be asked if they'd like to store their recordings on their device or through Google Drive. I suggest choosing Google Drive, which will allow them access to their recordings even when they are on a different device. **Sharing and submitting work** • Students can share their video through Classroom or Google Drive, or easily upload their creations to YouTube within the Screencastify extension.
FLIPGRID 	**Accessing the tool** • Students and teachers can access Flipgrid by downloading the app to their smartphone or by visiting flipgrid.com. **Student use** • After the teacher has shared the direct link to the grid or topic, students can easily respond to prompts and share their ideas with their peers and teacher. **Sharing and submitting work** • When students have finished recording their video, the recording is visible in the class topic or grid (unless the teacher chooses to keep the video private). Teachers can also share student responses through email, or embed code, a QR code, or a link to reach a wider audience.

Creating Video and Audio Products

IOS AND ANDROID CAMERA APPS	**Accessing the tool** • Students and teachers can access the camera app on an iOS or Android phone. **Student use** • Students can easily use their smartphone camera to quickly capture video for classroom purposes. Many students are already familiar with the camera on a smartphone or tablet, making preparation for using this tool simple or nonexistent. **Sharing and submitting work** • Students can easily share their recording with the teacher through email, or by adding the video to a drop box created by the teacher in Google Classroom.

CREATE VIDEO ACTIVITIES

Here are a few of the many kinds of activities you can design to encourage your students to show what they know, using video:

- **Amendments, laws, and court cases in action.** After studying landmark cases, constitutional amendments, or laws, students create skits showing what life would be like without those protections, or scenes that demonstrate what rights are protected because of them.
- **Video essays.** Instead of writing paragraph summaries or explanations, students create screencasts while verbally sharing their thoughts on the topic at hand.
- **Content review.** At the end of a chapter, study unit, or book, students create video reviews of a specific topic, theme, or standard. The videos can be posted throughout the classroom using QR codes or through Padlet or Google Classroom, allowing all students to access the resources created by their classmates.
- **Explaining answers.** Using video, students explain the thought process they followed to come up with the answer to a question or solve an equation. This activity not only helps students put their thought processes into words, it also helps the teacher better understand where any gaps or confusion in students' knowledge may be.
- **Commercials and public service announcements.** Students create video announcements and commercials to share information they've learned, describe how new or imaginative policies may be received by the public, or consider what life might be like without certain constitutional amendments, medicines, or inventions.

- **TED Talks.** After viewing examples of TED Talks, students deliver their own TED-style talks about content they have researched or are learning about in class. This is a great way for teachers to take advantage of the popularity of an event or activity to bring an authentic feel to classroom activities.

The possibilities for creating videos to demonstrate learning in the classroom are endless. In addition to providing students with an attractive option for showing what they've learned, video creation is a skill that students may need in their future careers. Creating videos to demonstrate learning is a great way for teachers to introduce and encourage their students to practice this skill.

SCAN THIS CODE TO SEE AN EXAMPLE OF A VIDEO CREATED WITH SCREENCASTIFY!

CREATING THROUGH PODCASTS

I fell head over heels in love with podcasts when I stumbled onto the *Presidential* podcast by the *Washington Post* during my commute to work. As a high school social studies teacher, it was right up my alley, and it helped to inspire me to start my own podcast—*Try This Tomorrow: Talks with Teachers*—to connect with other teachers on their commutes to work.

Turns out, podcasts can help inspire kids, too. When I asked my daughter Hanna if she wanted to add more reviews to her book blog (see chapter 3 for tips on starting a blog) while she did her summer reading, she said she wanted to try something different. Having seen me prepare my podcast, she thought she could do it too. Next thing we knew, her podcast, *Reading with Hanna*, was born.

By creating a podcast about the books she reads, Hanna is practicing important skills, including reading comprehension and summarization. She is also using technology as a medium to reach an audience. This has increased her excitement about putting together the podcast and her enthusiasm for the books she needs to read before creating each new episode. We've shared her podcast with the authors of the books she reads and have received wonderful, supportive comments from them. Imagine Hanna's surprise in discovering that the authors she reads listen to her reviews. There can't be much more positive reinforcement for a student's presentation skills than that.

Part of the beauty of creating a podcast is that it is incredibly easy to do and easy to share with a listening audience. There are many accessible platforms through which students and teachers can create their own podcasts to share what they're learning and demonstrate content understanding. Some of the choices include: Anchor (anchor.fm), Synth (gosynth.com), Screencastify (screencastify.com), and YouTube (youtube.com).

Creating Video and Audio Products

PODCAST CREATION TOOLS

ANCHOR

Access the tool
- Students can download the Anchor app using a smartphone or tablet, or access Anchor by visiting anchor.fm.

Student use
- Students can quickly create their own podcast by making an account (Anchor offers the ability to use a Google account to simplify the process), and then establishing a name for their podcast. When students are ready to record their first episode, they simply access the app on their smartphone and select the "record" icon at the bottom of the screen.

Sharing and submitting work
- When students have completed their recording, they can save the episode to their podcast or export the audio files to their device. Students can then easily share this file with their teacher through Google Drive, Google Classroom, or email.

SYNTH

Accessing the tool
- Students can create podcast episodes by downloading the Synth app on their smartphone or by accessing gosynth.com.

Student use
- Students can create a Synth account (Synth offers the ability to log in with a Google account) and then simply select the "+" icon, either on a smartphone/tablet, or at gosynth.com if they are using a computer.

Sharing and submitting work
- Students can submit or share their work by copying and pasting the link to their podcast. Students may also invite others to join their podcast by sharing an access code. Teachers can easily use this option to create a class podcast where the students contribute their ideas.

While Anchor and Synth allow students to create a podcast episode within their platforms, they also provide the option to upload existing audio files. Teachers and students can use Screencastify, YouTube, or the camera on their smartphone or tablet to create an audio file, download it to their device (doing so in Screencastify requires the premium version), and reupload it to Anchor or Synth.

 Create

CREATE PODCAST ACTIVITIES

- **Book talks.** Students contribute to a class podcast in which they share their reviews of books. Teachers share a list of the podcast's required components with their students and then encourage them to include additional "fun facts" or other information they find interesting about the book, genre, or author, or to make recommendations for who should read the book.
- **"If I were in charge . . ."** Students choose an important event or a decision made by a world leader and reflect upon that choice, discussing the pros and cons, as well as how the impact of that decision was felt by citizens. Students might also describe how they would have reacted when confronted by that decision. (Example: imagine being a woman in the 1970s during the equal rights movement and learning about the Equal Protection Clause of the Fourteenth Amendment.)
- **Important moments in history.** Students describe an important event, discovery, or contribution from the content they are studying as if they are sharing information with their peers. (Example: students could describe how the polio vaccine created by Jonas Salk or an electronic feeding device for amputees by Bessie Blount Griffin changed the world.)
- **STEM in school.** Students contribute to a podcast in which they share an experiment, creation, or design with the world. During their episode, students reflect on the process, their successes and failures, and the outcome of their activity.
- **Where in the world?** While participating in global collaboration projects, students choose to highlight a cultural component (daily life, typical meals, extracurricular activities), comparing and contrasting their own experiences with that of their partner school.

SCAN THIS CODE TO LISTEN TO MINUTES WITH MOLLY, A PODCAST BY MY SECOND GRADER!

 ## LEARN, CREATE, PRESENT, REPEAT

Getting over the awkwardness of making a presentation in front of an audience can be less painful for students when they learn to do it by putting their ideas across verbally through videos and podcasts. Once they experience how an audience reacts to their creations, confidence follows. Teachers can use technology tools to design activities in which their students create video and audio products that demonstrate their learning. This allows students to reflect upon and share their understanding of course content while practicing effective technology use.

TRY THIS TOMORROW

Scan the Screencastify QR code to add this great extension to your Chrome browser. Using the "share to Classroom" extension, push the Screencastify extension link to your students and direct them to add it to their browser. Encourage them to create a screencast in which they reflect upon a topic discussed in class. Have your students share their work with you using the option to save to Google Drive.

CREATING VIDEO AND AUDIO PRODUCTS: NOTES

3

Creating through Writing

GETTING THE WORDS DOWN IS KEY

No matter how technologically sophisticated we become or how visual we may be as communicators, we still have to learn to write. One way or another, we have to arrange words in a logical order so that we can express ourselves, answer questions, describe ideas, do research, tell stories, apply for scholarships, conduct business, and say what we mean—through writing.

As a student, I loved writing essays and research papers. English and history class assignments that required me to choose a topic, dive into primary and secondary sources, and then craft my own analysis of the research were my favorite means of demonstrating what I had learned. But not every student loves to write—or may not think they do—and many suffer through every essay they are assigned.

That's where the savvy teacher comes in. With the tools available today, we can introduce tech skills and activities that feel more like games than assignments, and that use creativity to make writing painless for the writing-averse. Of course, state, district, and content standards may require students to write research papers, and those things are important; but when students are given a choice in how they use their own words to demonstrate what they have learned, writing research papers becomes easier.

BLOGGING FOR TEACHERS AND STUDENTS

I started blogging in January of 2014 and immediately fell in love with the medium. My blog provides me with a platform through which to reflect on lessons and strategies and to brainstorm ideas for new projects and activities. Blogging also provides me an audience I can share with, and which will also hold me accountable for the quality of the learning experiences I design for my students. Blogs can be used for personal reflections, professional learning, and everything in between—including representations of student learning. For students, blogging about what they have learned also provides an opportunity to painlessly communicate using effective writing on a twenty-first-century platform, and to have their writing connect with an authentic audience.

BLOGGING CHOICES

Teachers have a range of websites to choose from when creating a blogging environment for students. Choices include spaces designed for education, such as edublogs (edublogs.org) or Kidblog (kidblog.org), as well as sites like Weebly and Blogger. Since many students are already familiar with Google Classroom and Padlet, these are also good choices for teachers interested in creating blogging opportunities.

BLOGGING TOOLS

PADLET

Accessing the tool
- Students and teachers can access Padlet through a web browser at padlet.com, or through an Android or iOS device via the app store. Teachers can select from a variety of templates, including grid or column designs, to create a class blog, and they are able to monitor student submissions and turn on a profanity filter.

Student use
- Students can respond to prompts posted by their teacher and comment on their classmates' posts. They can include videos, images, and other digital resources in their posts. (Scan the QR code for an example of a class blog.)

Submitting and sharing work
- To share their work, students simply respond to the prompt on the Padlet. Teachers and students can "react" to posts, and teachers can then share the Padlet through a link, QR code, or embed code.

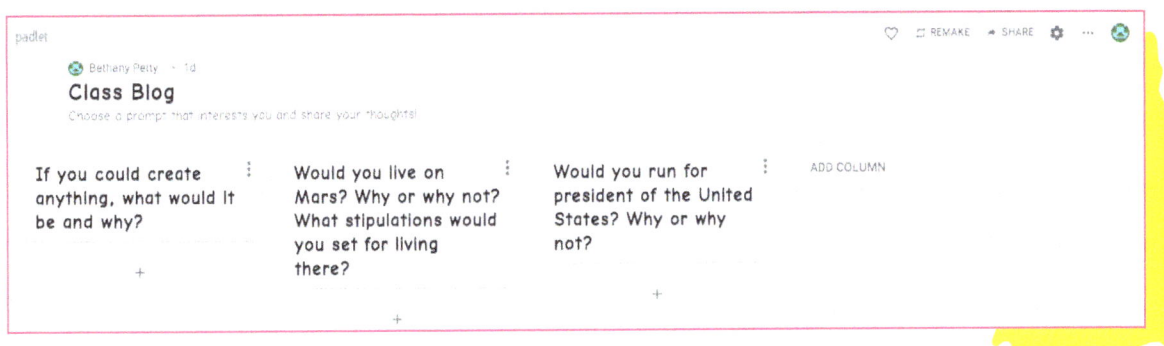

Create

GOOGLE CLASSROOM

Accessing the tool
- Students and teachers join Google Classroom (classroom.google.com) with a class code. Teachers create a specific Classroom section for class blog contributions. This provides a user-friendly space for students to collaborate across multiple class sections, and also helps teachers organize student contributions.

Student use
- After the teacher posts a blog prompt using the "question" option in Classroom, students respond to the question and, if the teacher allows this feature, to their classmates' posts.

Submitting and sharing work
- Students respond to questions assigned by their teacher and to their peers in a secure digital environment. Teachers can also respond and monitor student engagement, modeling social media etiquette and digital citizenship as they do.

USE THOSE WRITING SKILLS

Encourage students to create representations of what they've learned through blogging using:

Informative/explanatory writing:

- **Book blogs.** A different twist on the classic book report. Students become "book bloggers" by sharing their reviews of books they've read and recommending books to their peers.
- **Analyzing observations.** Students create a blog post in which they describe observations they make in developing a hypothesis.

Persuasive/argumentative writing:

- **Make a change.** After identifying a community or school issue, students blog about their proposed plan for solving the problem and lobby their peers, teachers, administrators, or local officials to support their ideas.
- **Contemporary issues bonus.** After researching a contemporary issue or event, students create a post on a class blog in which they share their opinion or a potential remedy for the issue in question.

WRITING WITH E-BOOKS

A few years ago, I started using "Show What You Know" bingo boards—also known as "choice boards"—in my classroom. I was tired of assigning and collecting exactly the same worksheet from every student. Students had no choice as to how they would share their knowledge; they just completed the worksheet, turned it in, got it back after I had graded it, and threw it away.

When I introduced Show What You Know to my students, I included an e-book option that they could use to demonstrate learning. By using a Google Slides presentation and reformatting the slide to 8.5" x 11", they were able to create a "book." Because it was an electronic book, students could include links to additional articles, videos, or games, and add their own originality to the project.

One of my students used Google Slides to create a series of e-books for children in which she described the foundations of government and the creation of the United States Constitution. It was wonderfully creative and more challenging than a traditional assignment. After I had evaluated the project and provided feedback, I created a QR code that linked to her e-books and posted it on the "Wall of Government Greatness" outside my classroom. Anyone who walked by could scan the code and view her work. She was able to choose what she wanted to create to demonstrate what she had learned and share it with an authentic audience.

E-BOOK WRITING CHOICES

Teachers and students can access a variety of tools, such as Canva (canva.com), Visme (visme.co), or Book Creator (bookcreator.com) to easily create e-books, or take advantage of the flexibility of Google Slides to accomplish this task.

A CLASSROOM OF AUTHORS

Students become authors when they're given the opportunity to create their own e-books to demonstrate what they've learned. Imagine the feeling of accomplishment your students will have when they share a book they have written.

Create

BOOK CREATION TOOLS

GOOGLE SLIDES

Accessing the tool
- Teachers can share a Google Slides e-book template with their students (scan the QR code in the table) through Google Classroom. Or, students create their own e-book template using Slides.

Student use
- Students can easily add and manipulate text boxes, images, videos, and links within a Google Slides presentation to create their own e-book.

Submitting and sharing work
- Students can share their e-book with their teacher and classmates or submit their work through Google Classroom.

BOOK CREATOR

Accessing the tool
- Teachers and students can access Book Creator (bookcreator.com) on an iPad or through their Chrome browser. While Book Creator does offer premium plans (starting at $60 per year per teacher for Chrome or $4.99 per subscription for iPad usage, at the time of this printing), teachers can create and share a library of up to forty books with their students for free.

Student use
- When teachers create a library through Book Creator, they share a code with their students, just as you would to add students to Google Classroom. Students can design the cover of their book with colors, images, or other backgrounds, and can add multiple pages that include their own text and images inserted from their device, Google Drive, Google Maps, or through a link/embed code.

Submitting and sharing work
- Students can submit their work to the teacher library, accessible to them through a teacher-provided code. Teachers then download books to share or print and can also publish student work online.

WRITING THROUGH TEXT MESSAGING

Think about how you interact with people through your phone. Do you make audio or video calls send text messages most often? Personally, I prefer to communicate through text, email, or social media. Audio or video calls are reserved for my husband, parents, sister, and nephew (who is currently two years old). I recently conducted an informal poll through Twitter, asking my fellow teachers how they most often use their phones for communication. The results were exactly what I expected—89 percent of respondents reported they communicate through texting, while 11 percent prefer to talk on their phones.

Most students probably also fall into the "texting over calling" category when they use cell phones. Teachers can take advantage of student familiarity with this form of communication by offering texting as an option for students to create products that demonstrate their understanding.

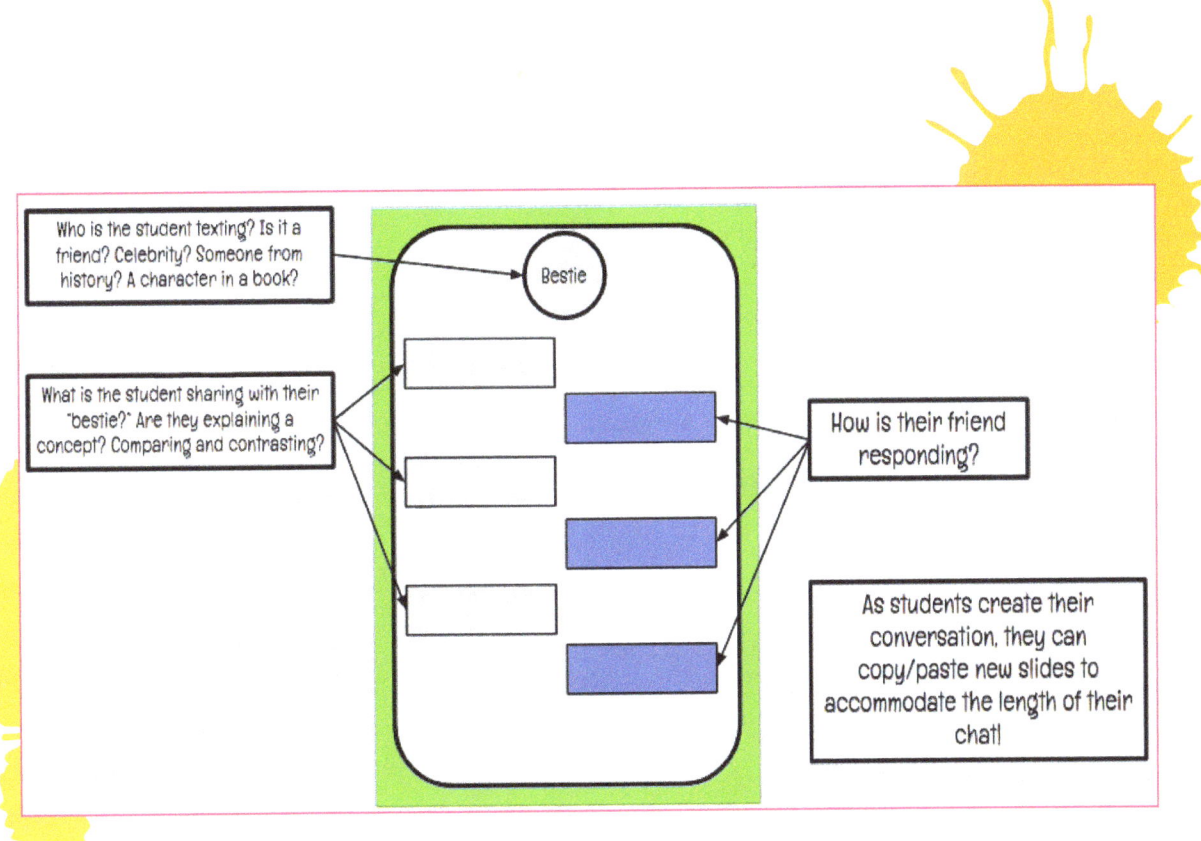

 *Create*

TEXT MESSAGE CREATION TOOLS

CLASSTOOLS

Accessing the tool
- Teachers and students can access the SMS text message creator at classtools.net (scan QR code).

Student use
- Students create conversations using the SMS message tool and save their work with a password and a unique URL. Be sure to let your students know that the floppy disk icon is the save button.

Submitting and sharing work
- Students can share their conversation with the teacher through email or Google Classroom.

GOOGLE SLIDES

Accessing the tool
- Scan the code to access a text message template. Teachers can make a copy of the template and assign it to their students using Google Classroom.

Student use
- Students can easily embed images and videos and add text to their conversation from anyone they choose, whether it be characters from a book, a period in history, or a famous scientist, poet, athlete, mathematician.

Submitting and sharing work
- Students can simply "turn in" this file if their teacher has assigned it through Google Classroom. Alternatively, students can easily embed their product on a Google site, share it with their teacher, or create a QR code that links to their creation.

So Many Ways to Get It—Write

There is no shortage of opportunities for students to use writing in creative ways to demonstrate what they have learned. As teachers, we have many digital tools available to encourage students to write and create products that allow them to take pride and ownership in their work.

WRITING WEB PAGES AND CREATING WEBSITES

Our students are no strangers to using websites for gathering information, but they can also easily create and publish web pages to demonstrate learning. Students can create websites using a variety of tools, such as Adobe Spark or Google Sites, and include text, images, links, and videos to illustrate their understanding.

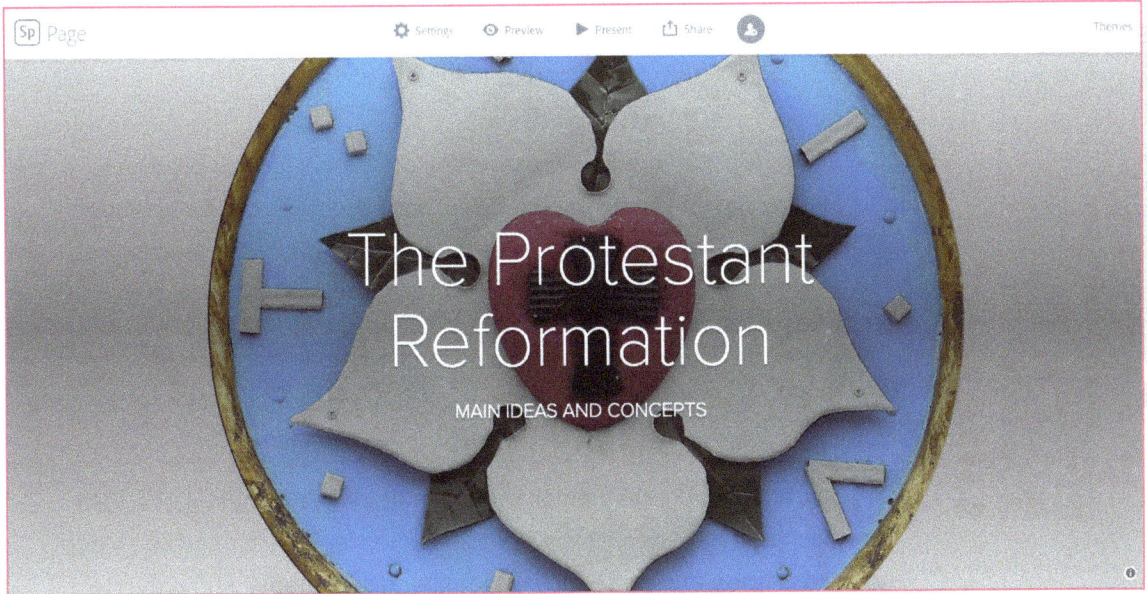

Using Adobe Spark, students can create a presentation that functions as a web page and easily share their published work via email, social media, link, or Google Classroom. They can also collaborate with their peers during the creation process.

USING WEB PAGES TO DEVELOP WRITING SKILLS

- **Databases of learning.** Students work individually or collaboratively to create websites that serve as a database or a portfolio of learning. These databases might include the students' research and analysis of anything related to class content, for example: landmark Supreme Court cases, tips for future classes, examples of hypotheses in action.
- **Public service announcements.** Students create a website that provides information on a contemporary issue. The site might include a variety of digital resources offering multiple perspectives on the issue, video explanations of the issue, as well as personal opinions.

TEXT MESSAGE CREATION TOOLS

ADOBE SPARK

Accessing the tool
- Teachers and students can access Adobe Spark by visiting spark.adobe.com and signing in with a Google account.

Student use
- Students can create videos, images, or web pages using Adobe Spark and embed images, links, and other digital media.

Submitting and sharing work
- Students can share their creations by downloading their product to their device or by sharing the URL. These products can be uploaded to Google Classroom to be accessed and shared by the teacher.

GOOGLE SITES

Accessing the tool
- Teachers and students can access the new, user-friendly version of Google Sites by going to sites.google.com/new, or by scanning the code.

Student use
- Students can create their own website or blog and share it with their teacher, classmates, or with a wider audience. They can embed video and images, and add text, links to other digital media, and pages to their website.

Submitting and sharing work
- Students can share their website URL with the teacher and can submit their site through Google Classroom. Teachers and students can create QR codes directing others to students' sites, which can then be displayed in the classroom or around the school building.

TRY THIS TOMORROW

Create a "class blog" using Google Classroom to encourage students to share their thoughts in writing on a variety of topics. Create a specific section dedicated solely to this blog and share the code with students who wish to participate. This provides students with a dedicated platform not only to share their ideas and opinions in writing, but also to practice digital citizenship in a safe environment.

CREATING THROUGH WRITING: NOTES

Creating with Games

PLAYING GAMES TAKES BRAINS

Imagine yourself as a student once again—you pick the age. You're sitting at your desk, awaiting a boring assignment when, instead, your teacher gives you the option to create and play a game to demonstrate that you have understood the content. Suddenly you're interested, but games are interesting for the teacher too.

In many of today's classrooms, students play games like Kahoot, Quizizz, and Quizlet Live for formative assessment after a lesson, or to review material for a test. Data from these games provides teachers with very informative insights about student learning that can be used to drive instruction. Students review course information while participating in these game-based assessment activities, and have fun doing so because of the competitive natures of the games; they feel less like school assignments and more like activities they might do with friends. But in addition to playing games created by their teachers, students can get creative, developing games of their own to show what they are learning.

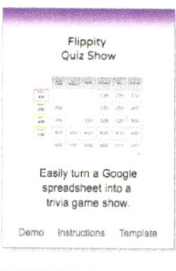

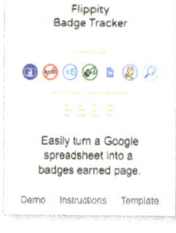

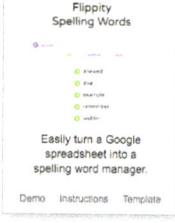
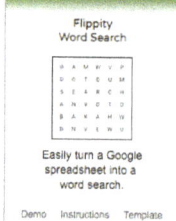

Before I decide to try a new strategy, tool, or lesson in my classroom, I always ask myself one simple question: Why? Why am I trying this strategy? Is it going to make learning more engaging for my students? Is using this tool going to allow my students to demonstrate their learning in a different way? In creating games to show what they understand about a subject, students are thinking about the content they've covered in class, and they display what they've learned by formulating questions and response options.

Providing students with creative choices helps them to engage more fully in what they are learning, and in the way they wish to demonstrate that knowledge. By giving students the opportunity to play a game they created with their peers, we encourage them to share their learning with each other, as well as with us.

TOOLS FOR CREATING GAMES

FLIPPITY

Accessing the tool
- Students and teachers can access Flippity through the website (flippity.net) or by using the Flippity add-on in Google Sheets.

Student use
- Students can easily create a wide variety of games using Flippity, including game show–style activities, digital bingo cards, matching games, and crossword puzzles.

Submitting and sharing work
- When students create games using Flippity, they work with Google Sheets and can quickly share their spreadsheet with the teacher. After students publish their spreadsheet, they're able to view the activity they created on the web and share the link with their teacher and peers.

QUIZIZZ

Accessing the tool
- Students can create games with Quizizz by visiting quizizz.com and creating an account. Quizizz offers the ability to sign up using a Google account.

Student use
- Students create quiz-style games and can include images and text, as well as mathematical functions in their questions. Questions can include multiple correct answers, and responses are followed by memes.

Submitting and sharing work
- After publishing their game, students can share their work with their teacher and peers through a link or through social media tools.

QR CODE GAME (GOOGLE SHEETS)

Accessing the tool

- Students can access the extension by going to the "add-ons" menu in Google Sheets, searching for and selecting the QR Code Generator, and then adding it to their spreadsheet.

Student use

- When students are ready to create their QR code game, they simply enter the information (definitions, terms, facts, review concepts) into their spreadsheet and run the add-on. In my classroom, students include the term or concept in the column that will become the QR code and a description or explanation in the next column.

Submitting and sharing work

- Students can submit their work to Google Classroom or print their QR codes to share with classmates.

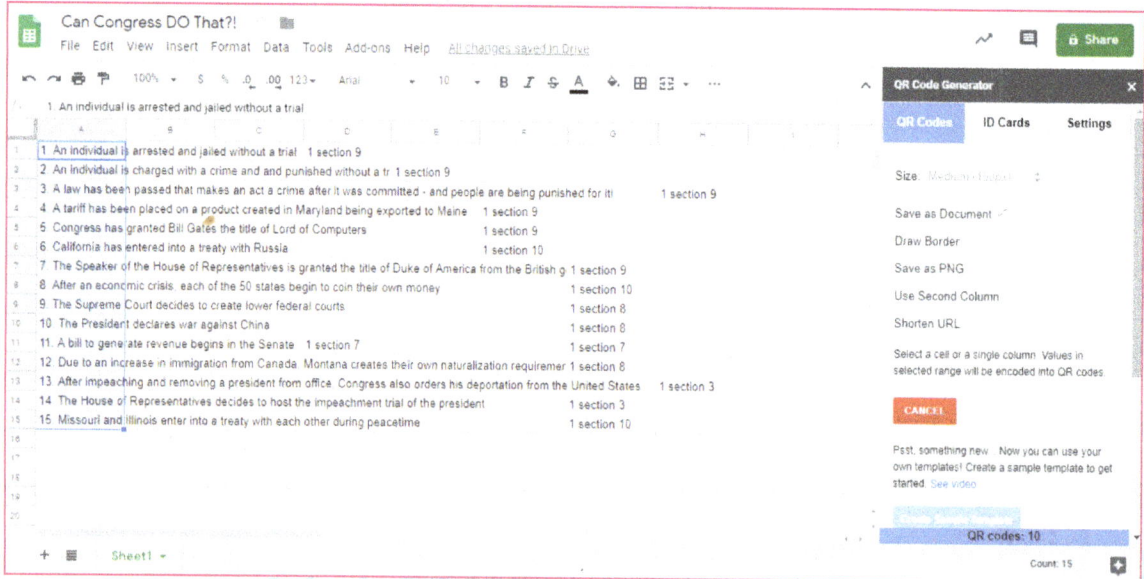

LOW-TECH/NO-TECH GAMES

While Flippity and Quizizz offer students many choices for creating games to demonstrate learning, teachers can also take advantage of many "low-tech" or "no-tech" options.

A favorite low-tech option in my classroom is "Constitution-opoly," a board game I created to help my students review for their Constitution test. In Missouri, students must pass a US Constitution test in order to graduate from high school. This obviously creates quite a bit of stress, but playing this game helps my students not only to review the content, but also to have fun doing so. Although I designed the game specifically for my high school government class, the template can easily be used in any content area and grade level. Students can also edit this template to create their own content-specific games to share with their peers.

Although the low-tech games Constitution-opoly, Show What You Know, and Facepalm, listed below, are created using technology (Google Slides), they are played in the classroom without the use of devices.

LOW-TECH GAMES

"-OPOLY" GAMES

Accessing the tool
- Teachers can access the "-opoly" game template by scanning this QR code. They can then create a copy of the template and share it with their students through Google Classroom.

Student use
- Students can easily create "-opoly" games by editing the template the teacher shared with them. They then use Google Images to locate different "pieces" for the game based on what they are studying.

Submitting and sharing work
- Students can submit their work through Google Classroom and print their game to share with their classmates.

Create

SHOW WHAT YOU KNOW 	**Accessing the tool** • Teachers can access this game template by scanning the QR code. They can then create a copy of the template, edit to fit the needs of their students, and share it with students through Google Classroom. **Student use** • Students can edit the cards to reflect the topic they are studying, adjusting the point values and actions as needed. **Submitting and sharing work** • If the Show What You Know game is assigned through Classroom, students can simply submit their assignment. Teachers and students can then print and cut out the completed activities (printing four slides per page) to share the game with the class.
FACEPALM 	**Accessing the tool** • Teachers can access the Facepalm game template by scanning the QR code. They can then create a copy, edit the template, and share it with their students through Google Classroom. **Student use** • Students can edit the term cards, as well as the "tip card," to fit the content they are learning. **Submitting and sharing work** • If the game is assigned through Google Classroom, students may simply submit their work digitally.

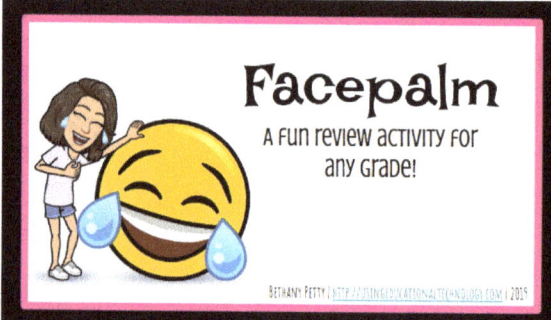

CREATING GAMES TO DEMONSTRATE LEARNING

- **Extension activities.** In my American Government classes, I offer my students extension opportunities with each unit. Students are able to choose how they demonstrate what they've learned, and one of the options is to create a game. Students work on this game throughout our unit, reflecting on information and adding new details as they progress through our content.
- **Presentation review.** When students present information to their peers, they can create a game for their classmates to complete at the end of the presentation. This is beneficial to the student giving the presentation because the game serves as a check on their own understanding. The game is also helpful for their classmates because they are able to review the content they learned through the presentation.
- **Introducing content to new or younger students** When students complete a unit or review for an assessment, they can create a game that not only serves as a review activity for their peers, but also introduces future students to the content. In creating this activity, students reflect on what they've read and think about how to explain the content in different ways.

Smart Gaming

Devising a game about course content that is clever enough to challenge their peers is a sure-fire means for a student to show what they know. Playing games they've created is a fun and meaningful learning experience for our students.

Too often in my classroom, I worry that my students are so accustomed to the way I ask questions that they look for clues in the questions in order to come up with the answers. But when they play games their peers have created, my students are being exposed to and thinking about the content in different ways. When our students create products for an audience, especially if they are sharing their work with their peers, the quality of their work increases. No one wants to share subpar work with the world.

TRY THIS TOMORROW

Scan the Facepalm code to access the template. Edit the cards and share the template with your students through Google Classroom. Encourage them to create their own version of the game to share with the class on test review day.

CREATING WITH GAMES: NOTES

5
Creating with Visual Aids

DON'T FORGET LOW-TECH—A PENCIL AND PAPER ARE OPTIONS, TOO

While the increasing availability of technology in the classroom is providing amazing learning opportunities for teachers and students, it's important to remember that our focus as teachers should be on student learning rather than the technology we use. Classroom technology should provide teachers and students with options, not another mandate.

When my students are preparing projects to show what they've learned, I try to provide them with a variety of creative options, some traditional and some quite different. I also encourage them to share new product ideas with me if they would rather create their project by some means other than the ones I've suggested. Many of my students navigate toward screencasts, essays, or games, but as I was giving an overview for one assignment, a student asked, "Can I make something with paper?"

Of course!

As a teacher in the classroom today, I sometimes assume that my students will automatically *want* to work with technology. But, while technology provides students with a wealth of opportunities to learn and demonstrate their understanding, it's important for teachers to step back and ask, "What's driving my technology integration? Am I using technology because I have to, or am I using it to provide my students with more options to enhance their learning?"

USING BOARD TIME TO DEMONSTRATE LEARNING

Not using technology can be just as effective as using it. I recently made a change in my classroom in an effort to give students more opportunities to collaborate with their peers to demonstrate what they have learned; we call this BOARD time. Here's how it breaks down:

BRAINSTORM, "OH!", ANALYZE, REVIEW AND REFLECT, DISCUSS AND DRAW = BOARD

 *Create*

Our class participates in BOARD time sporadically throughout our class period, depending on the content and responses from their "evidence of learning forms" (**ELFs**).

During the **brainstorm** portion, students write or draw on their whiteboard with a dry-erase marker and propose new constitutional amendments, share ideas or solutions to historical and modern problems, share prior knowledge about a concept or event, and list lingering questions about content.

The **"Oh!"** section of BOARD time encourages students to react when they learn something new. This component asks students to discuss things that surprise them with their peers, and to record those things on their group whiteboard. These might be things that the students learned from a flipped video (video created by the teacher or shared from another source to deliver instruction), an article, or a discussion—anything that made them open their minds to ideas and possibilities they had never considered before, or that made them change their minds.

SCAN THIS CODE TO LEARN HOW TO USE AN ELF IN YOUR CLASSROOM!

The **analyze** component provides my students with an opportunity to work with their peers to analyze primary and secondary sources, political cartoons, charts, graphs, and other information. They create questions about the documents they work with, discuss the point of view of the authors and/or illustrators, and share their thoughts with their peers.

The **review and reflect** portion of BOARD time may be my favorite. My students use this opportunity not only to think about what they have learned through an activity, but also to share these insights with their peers. The conversations that I overhear during BOARD time, particularly through **review and reflect,** provide me with amazing feedback on instruction. Walking around my classroom and listening to my students respond to a certain prompt, I quickly learn about points of confusion that I need to address with the class or with individuals.

The final component of BOARD time, probably my students' favorite, is **discuss and draw.** Students are encouraged to discuss different ways to share the information they've learned with their peers. When the group has fleshed out their thoughts and has a clear understanding of the content, they create a nonverbal representation of a concept, event, or document to demonstrate what they've learned. The drawings my students share with the class are fantastic! They're able to demonstrate their understanding of content and have fun doing so.

Effective Low-Tech

BOARD time is a great example of how students can work together to create representations of what they have learned in class, without using their Chromebook, iPad, smartphone, or a website. Technology is a tool for the classroom, not a requirement for learning.

CREATING VISUAL AIDS TO DEMONSTRATE LEARNING

The increasing availability of technology has provided teachers and students with nearly infinite possibilities and options for creating visual aids to demonstrate learning. The following strategies can be used in classrooms with any level of technology accessibility.

ONE-PAGERS

While originally developed as a tool for English and language arts classes, a one-pager can be used across the curriculum to demonstrate content understanding. A one-pager, as its name implies, is a single piece of paper that includes multiple components based on the content of the course. One-pagers, which are similar to a Frayer model vocabulary activity, require students to include or explain an element of the content they're learning using a variety of examples: textual sources, modern/personal life, information from news media outlets, and images (created by the student or drawn from digital resources).

One-pagers provide students with the opportunity to explain what they have learned from a novel, an instructional video, a primary source, a lecture, or another class activity. The exercise requires students to reflect on their own understanding while providing examples from multiple sources. Students are also able to express their creativity visually through the use of images, creative lettering, colors, and other artistic components.

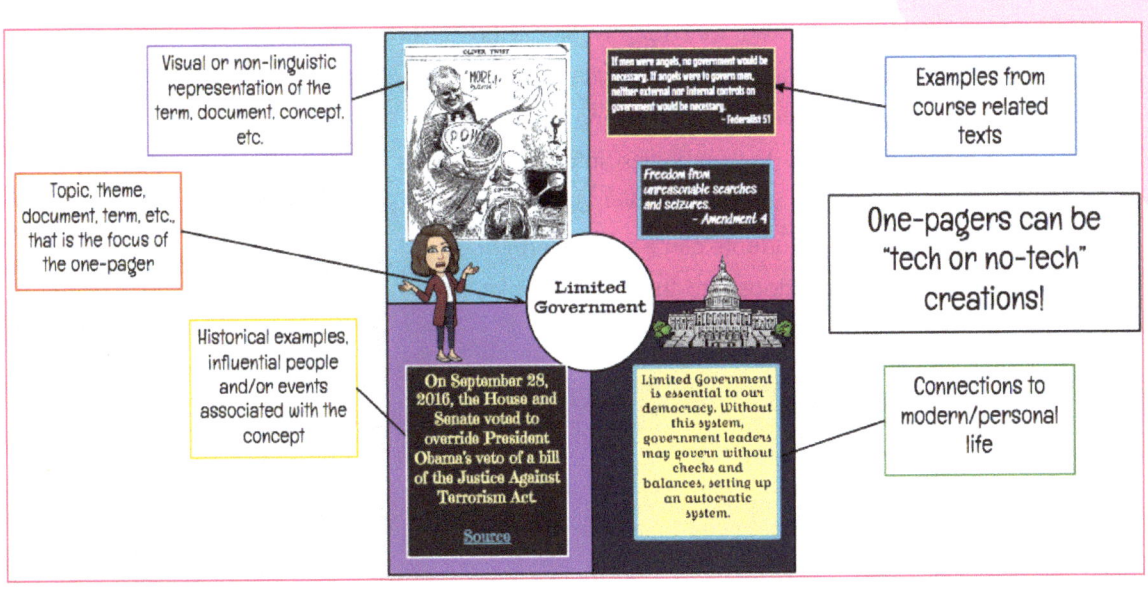

 *Create*

USING ONE-PAGERS IN THE CLASSROOM

- **Visualizing vocabulary.** Students create a one-pager to deeply describe a vocabulary term or an important concept they're learning about in class. The various components of a one-pager can help students form a more thorough understanding of a concept.
- **Describing themes.** In an ELA classroom, students might create a one-pager to demonstrate their understanding of a theme or main idea in the text they're reading in class. When designing the one-pager, teachers can easily tie the various components to commonly assessed ELA standards, such as drawing references from texts to support a claim or idea.
- **Character analysis.** Students create a one-pager to describe the evolution of a character in a novel or film. When designing the components of the one-pager, teachers can tailor the requirements to fit the style of the text and the standards addressed during the activity.

INFOGRAPHICS

To spice up a unit on economics, I suggested that my students use infographics to demonstrate what they had learned. But to my surprise, they had never heard of an infographic. "It's kind of like a poster that you would make, with charts, images, and a few words, to explain a concept," I explained. As soon as I said, "poster," sounds of, "Oh, OK," floated to the front of my classroom.

While this explanation worked well for my students, I hesitate to describe an infographic as a digital poster, because it can be so much more. When creating an infographic, our students are able to synthesize information they have learned and present content in a well-organized and easy-to-understand way. Students can easily insert QR codes, embedded links, and videos into their infographics to add another form of explanation to their product.

CREATIVE WAYS TO USE INFOGRAPHICS

- **Contrast perspectives.** Students create an infographic to contrast perspectives on contemporary or historical issues.
- **Career requirements and trends.** After researching a potential career, students create an infographic

to illustrate the education requirements, job-related skill experience, projected openings, and salary.

- **Research presentation.** Instead of creating a typical presentation using Slides or a comparable tool, students create an infographic that illustrates their findings and conclusions about a topic they are researching.

PLAYING CARDS

Creating a traditional presentation to demonstrate understanding is one option for students, but asking them to create playing cards to illustrate what they are learning adds a fun element to the assignment, while still allowing teachers to assess relevant standards.

I created a trading card template as an extension activity a few years ago when my American Government students were studying the powers of the executive branch. There is never enough time to go into this subject thoroughly, but I still wanted to give my students the opportunity to learn about presidential history and have fun doing while doing it.

Students were able to choose any former president for this activity. While they looked for information on such topics as "rivals," "teammates," and "career stats," they were actually conducting research, evaluating information, and assessing the contributions of leaders throughout history, all while effectively using technology to demonstrate learning.

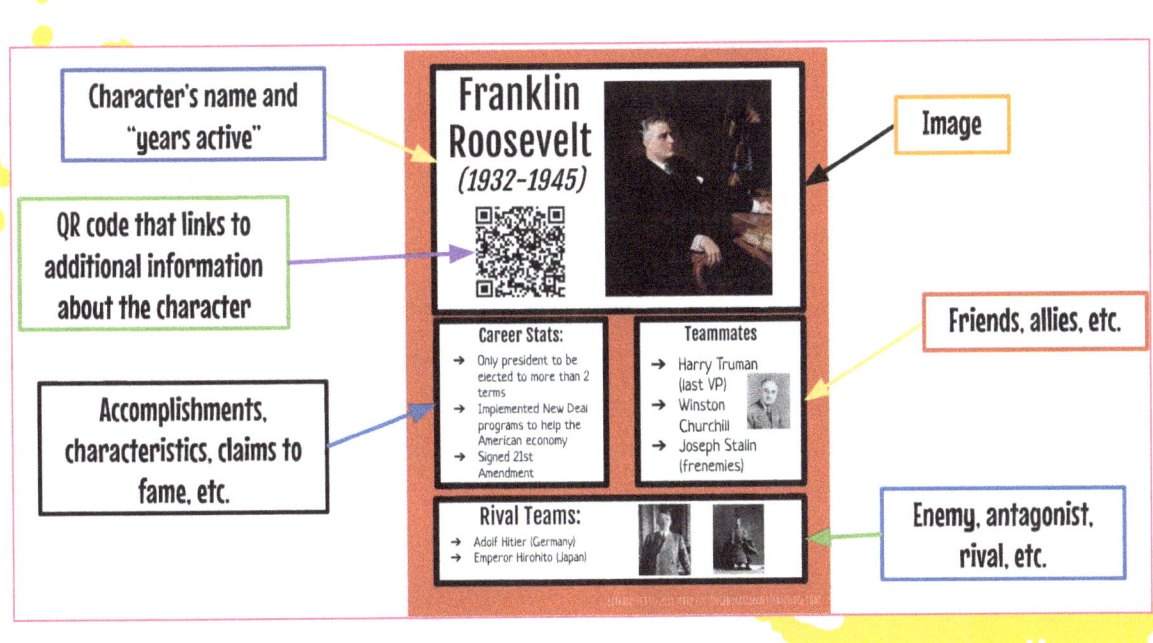

CARD GAMES FOR SAVVY STUDENTS

Although I developed this activity for my high school social studies class, it can easily be adapted for other content areas and grade levels.

- **Essential Elements.** Create an executive branch version of the periodic table of elements. Students create an "Essential Element" card (in the style of the president card above) in which they describe the element, list common compounds (for "teammates" or "claims to fame"), compounds that are dangerous to humans ("rivals"), and facts about the element ("career stats").
- **Character cards.** While reading a novel or other literary work, students develop a "character card" to describe a protagonist, antagonist, or supporting player from the story.
- **Current Events.** Students create a "Current Events" card to describe multiple perspectives of a contemporary issue or provide more information about an individual associated with an event.

TOOLS AND TEMPLATES FOR CREATING VISUAL AIDS	
ONE-PAGERS 	**Accessing the tool** • Students and teachers can access a template for creating a one-pager by scanning the QR code. **Student use** • Students can create their one-pager by editing the digitally assigned template from the teacher, or may print the template to create work using other resources. **Submitting and sharing work** • Students can easily submit and share their work through Google Classroom.
INFOGRAPHICS 	**Accessing the tool** • Students and teachers can use a variety of tools to create infographics. Scan the code or access canva.com to create a free account. **Student use** • Students can edit an existing template on Canva to create their infographic or start from scratch. **Submitting and sharing work** • Students can submit their infographic as a link to Google Classroom. Teachers can easily print the infographic or create a QR code that links to student work for display.

TRADING CARDS 	**Accessing the tool** • Teachers can access this template by scanning the QR code, and can then assign the template to their students using Google Classroom, or print it and provide it to their students in class. **Student use** • Students can create their playing cards digitally or without the use of technology. Instead of searching for an image, students can draw their character, letting their creativity shine. **Submitting and sharing work** • Students can submit their work through Google Classroom.

SKETCHNOTING

Visual note-taking, or sketchnoting, is becoming increasingly popular in the world of education. I introduced my students to sketchnoting a few years ago as a way to illustrate the requirements and due dates for a HyperDoc unit we were completing. Students responded well to this sketchnote and referenced it frequently throughout the unit, so I casually mentioned that they could sketchnote their extension activities. The immediate response was "But I can't draw."

Fortunately, you don't need to be an amazing artist to create visual representations of learning. On her website, sketchnoting guru Sylvia Duckworth, the author of two books on the subject, shares a wealth of resources related to the benefits of using visual note-taking and a more intentional form of doodling to help students form meaningful connections to what they are learning. Be sure to check out Sylvia's work at sylviaduckworth.com.

Through sketchnoting, students combine a mix of words and images not only to help them visualize learning, but also to help make information stick.

SKETCHNOTING AND INTENTIONAL DOODLING IDEAS

- **Show the flow.** Students can create sketchnotes to demonstrate continuity in virtually any subject: the steps involved in solving an equation, the process through which a bill becomes a law, how timelines of important events fall into place, or the phases of cellular division.
- **If-then .** Students illustrate a cause-and-effect relationship through sketchnoting. For example, "If Americans reduce their dependence on foreign oil, then . . ." Or, "If a border wall is constructed between Mexico and the United States, then . . ." The possibilities are endless.
- **Reading reviews.** In another take on a book report, students choose to create a sketchnote of a chapter, character, or event from a book they have read.

 Create

I reached out to renowned sketchnoter, Julie Woodard, to create a visual of a chapter from my first book, *Illuminate: Technology Enhanced Learning*. She not only captured the message of the chapter, but also provided an excellent example of sketchnoting!

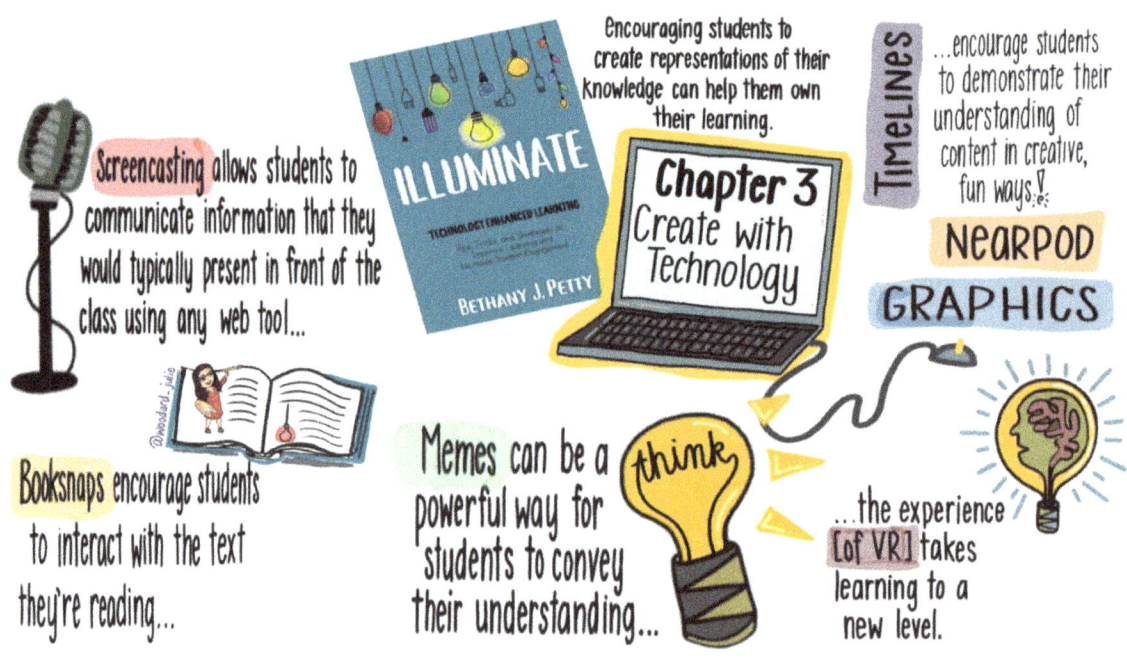

SAY IT IN PICTURES

Creating visual aids is a fun and effective way for students to demonstrate what they have learned, and there are many options for doing so, utilizing Chromebooks, iPads, cell phones, markers, pens, and paper. Remember that the technology in our classrooms opens our students to new possibilities when creating representations of knowledge, but using technology to create these products is not a requirement for learning. It's not about the tech; it's how we use it to enhance learning.

> ### TRY THIS TOMORROW
> Scan the code to download the one-pager template. Edit the template and then assign it to your students via Google Classroom as a vocabulary activity. Encourage your students to create their one-pager with or without technology, to be creative, and to have fun demonstrating what they know!

CREATING WITH VISUAL AIDS: NOTES

6

Evaluating Creations

THE CHALLENGE OF DIFFERENTIATION

Differentiating instruction is one of the most challenging aspects of teaching, but it's also one of the most important. As teachers, we know that our students do not all learn the same way. We also know that many of our students probably don't learn the way we learned, which can make it tricky to develop activities with differentiation in mind.

As a student, particularly in middle and high school, I was a fan of "sit-and-get" lecture-style classes. When it came time to demonstrate what I had learned, I loved to write essays and papers because written response activities worked best for me and my learning style. When I started teaching, I wanted to use these same instructional strategies in my classroom. I wasn't ready to venture outside my comfort zone and the bounds of the lecture-worksheets-study guides-test cycle (with maybe a foldable thrown in here or there). I eventually learned, fortunately, that growth and improvement don't happen in comfort zones.

I knew that my students needed differentiation, and while I had great ideas for lessons that would help my students learn and apply content, I had one major hang-up: How in the world would I grade differentiated assignments?

Rubrics were the best answer for the activities that my students were completing, but the rubrics I had created early in my career were not useful at all. This contributed to my fear of differentiating instruction, because I knew I wasn't evaluating student work based on the learning targets, and I didn't know how to fix it.

When I started offering my students more choice in how they demonstrate learning, I found myself scrambling to create a rubric for each project option I gave my students. The problem there, however, was that I was using these rubrics not to evaluate my students progress in relation to learning targets, but to determine whether or not they had completed the assignment. My criteria were vague, the descriptors were confusing and wordy, and none of the information was presented in student-friendly language. Rubrics should be tied to and truly evaluate whether or not student work has met a learning standard.

My students were unclear on the requirements for projects, and while I went over the rubric with my students, I wasn't taking the time to thoroughly explain the rubric's criteria and descriptors. I didn't provide my students with examples of work at the various levels of the rubric. I didn't encourage them to frequently assess their own work to gain an understanding of what information they needed to add to reach their goal.

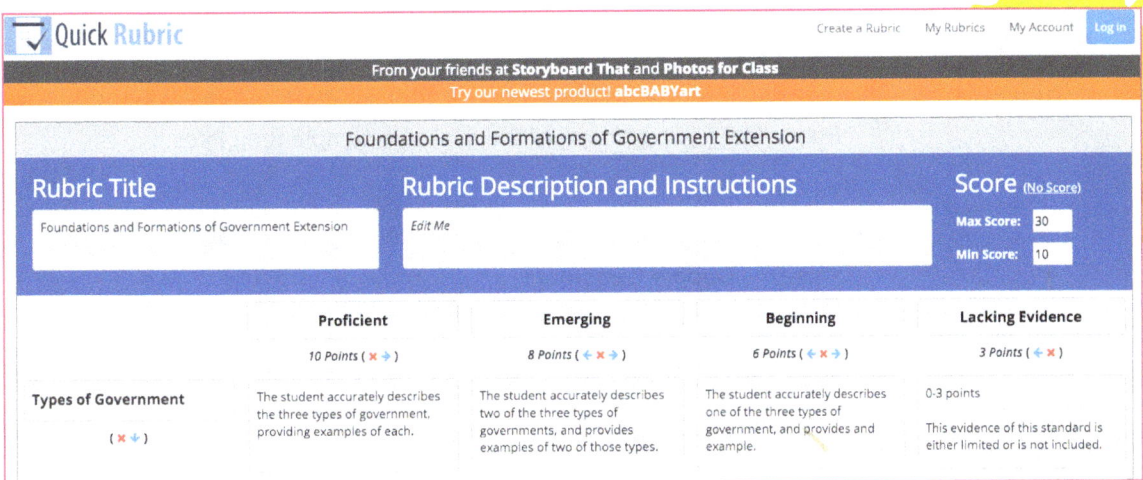

The more I learned about how to evaluate student work and provide effective feedback related to learning targets, the better my rubrics became.

My school district, through an instructional leadership program for teachers, began to research and apply the conclusions of the work of John Hattie, Nancy Frey, and Douglas Fisher on effective learning practices. As part of this team, my main focus was learning about implementing and sharing my experiences with the strategy known alternately as ACL (assessment-capable learners) or DACL (developing assessment-capable learners).

Assessment-capable learners are students who are familiar with frequent self-assessment and with monitoring where they are in their learning. They understand where they are going in terms of mastering learning targets, and they know what they need to do in order to reach the goals they have established for themselves.

As part of this instructional leadership program (and after learning about the positive impact the strategy could have on my classroom), I knew that I needed to dive into it head first. As a social studies teacher who frequently uses projects and rubrics to facilitate student learning, implementing this strategy would force me to develop effective rubrics that clearly communicated expectations tied to learning standards.

Teachers can quickly and easily create rubrics tailored specifically to their students using readily available tools such as Google Docs, Slides, Forms, and Sheets. Other free tools including Rubistar,

Quick Rubric, and a new update from Google Classroom that makes creating effective rubrics that are tied to course standards a breeze.

FREE TOOLS FOR CREATING RUBRICS	
RUBRIC MAKER 	**Accessing the tool** • Teachers can access Rubric Maker at rubric-maker.com, or by scanning the QR code. **Teacher use** • Teachers can easily create rubrics for their students from scratch using Rubric Maker, or edit one of the available sample templates. **Sharing with students** • Teachers can print rubrics for their students or download the rubric to share via Google Classroom.
QUICK RUBRIC 	**Accessing the tool** • Teachers can access Quick Rubric by visiting quickrubric.com, or by scanning the QR Code. **Teacher use** • Teachers can quickly create rubrics with Quick Rubric by signing up for an account using the Google single sign-on. Rubrics are easily edited to meet the needs of students. **Sharing with Students** • Rubrics made with Quick Rubric can be downloaded and printed to share with students, or shared with a unique URL to Google Classroom.

A GREAT NEW TOOL

In the summer of 2019, Google released an extremely useful update to Classroom that allows teachers to add a customized rubric to any assignment. This is slowly being made available to all teachers who use Google Classroom. To add a rubric to an assignment in Google Classroom, simply create an assignment and click "create rubric." You'll be given the option to create a rubric with or without point values and can add multiple criteria, levels, and descriptors to clarify expectations.

To evaluate student work with the rubric, teachers simply open the student file and select the grading icon to access the rubric. Teachers will then see the grading criteria they included in the rubric and can provide immediate and individualized feedback through the comment feature.

Evaluating Creations

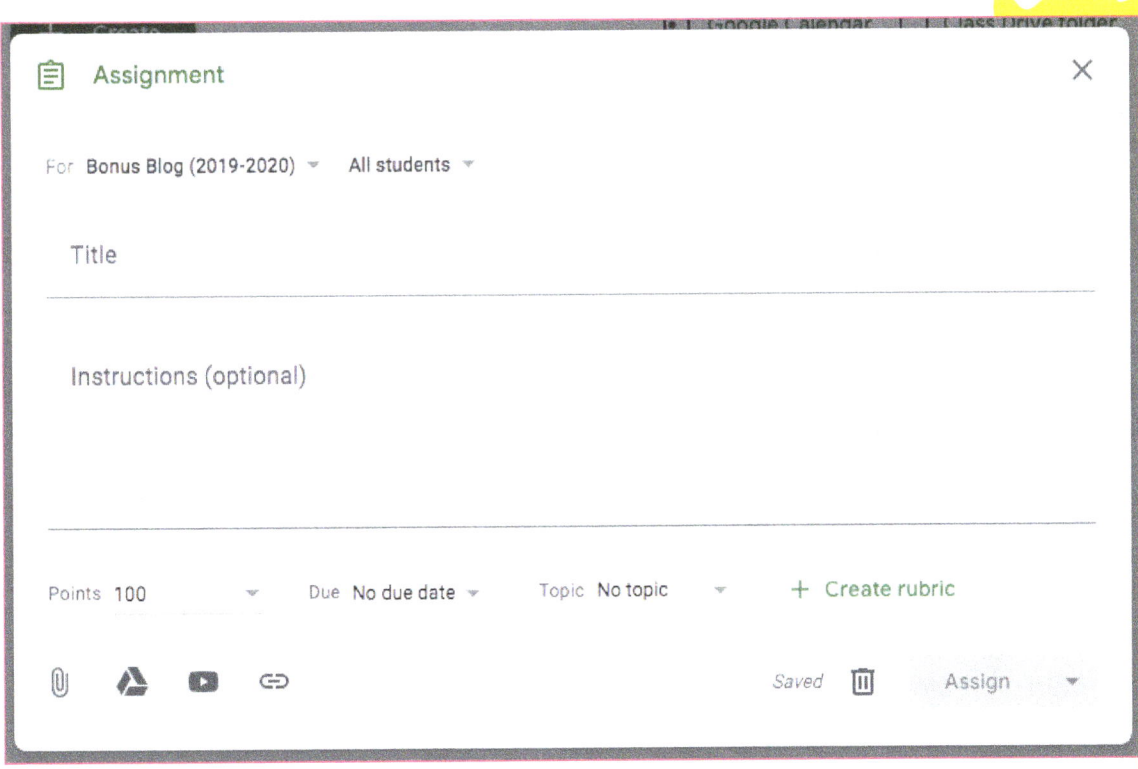

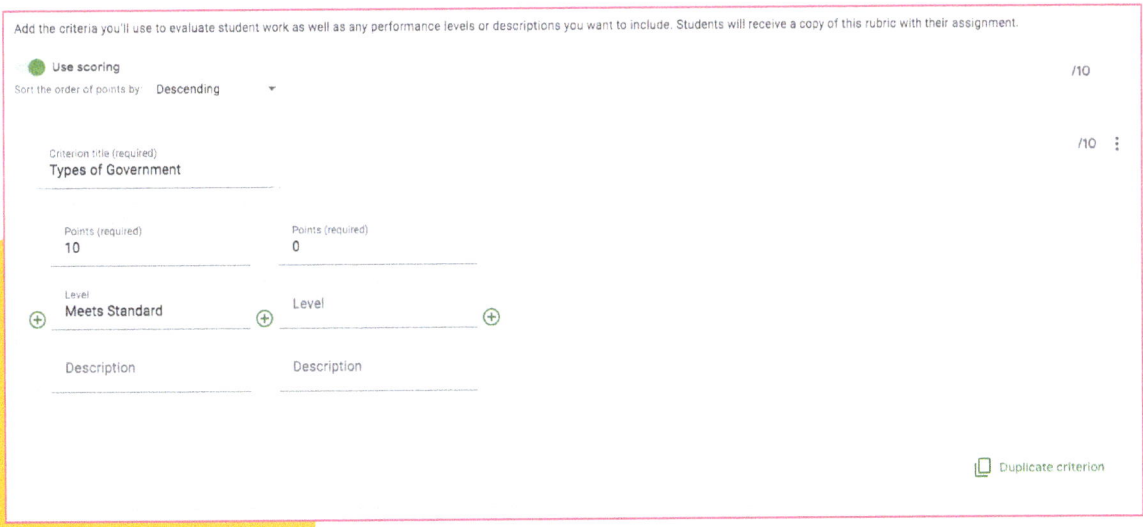

Create

No matter which tool you choose to use to create rubrics to evaluate student projects, it's important to remember to develop rubrics that clearly explain the requirements for creations and that are tied to course and/or content-level standards.

FREQUENT SELF-ASSESSMENT OF LEARNING

I frequently deliver seminars that focus on effective use of technology in the classroom. Before I leave for these workshops, I always poll my students, asking them what kind of feedback, from their perspective, I should share with other teachers.

Recently, the biggest "be sure to tell them" concern that my students wanted me to pass along has been about using frequent formative assessment to drive instruction. Of course, my students didn't use the phrase "frequent formative assessment" in their discussion. Instead, they said, "tell them to use Kahoot and Quizizz all the time, not just right before the test."

Without knowing it, my students were describing the importance of frequent formative assessment and self-reflection in the learning process. They hit the nail on the head, so to speak, by recognizing how important these things are in helping them as learners, and helping their teacher, too.

While my students mentioned formative assessment games, using rubrics to frequently self-assess is also effective. When students are introduced to a project, the rubric typically accompanies the information and requirements. But how often do we give students the opportunity to assess themselves?

Until about two years ago, I didn't encourage or give my students the opportunity to intentionally self-assess or reflect on the products they were creating. I introduced the project, briefly went over the rubric, and then we got to work. The next time my students interacted with the project rubric was when I returned it to them—with my comments and their grade.

Fast forward to today. My students frequently self-assess using the rubric when they are creating projects that demonstrate learning. They can highlight the criteria that fit their project in each phase of creation. They have a clear understanding, based on their own reflection, of where they are in the learning process, where they are going in regard to the end goal, and how to get there. As their teacher, it's amazing for me to watch them critically evaluate their product based on our learning standards. Just as the results of the summative assessment should not be a surprise for teachers, the score a student earns for a creation that demonstrates learning should be clear and understood.

> ### TRY THIS TOMORROW
> Encourage your students to frequently assess their own learning through project rubrics that are tied to learning standards.

EVALUATING CREATIONS: NOTES

7
Sharing Creations

Think back to your student years again. Your teacher has just given you an assignment to create something that demonstrates your understanding of course content, whether that be an essay, a poster, a PowerPoint presentation, a board game, or any other project. In addition to the project requirements, your teacher provides you with a rubric, and you clearly understand what is expected of you when you submit your assignment.

You know the only person who will view your project is your teacher. You also know that as soon as the teacher returns the graded assignment to you, it will find a new home stuffed in a drawer in your room, piled with a bunch of other projects kept by your parents, or crumpled in the trash. With this knowledge, you create your project.

Imagine how much more effort and pride you would put into your creations if you knew your work would reach an authentic audience. What if your work would be shared as a sample of your abilities? What if your peers were able to view your work? When we create products for the world to see, we want that work to be awesome!

AN AUDIENCE BEYOND THE CLASSROOM

When teachers design environments and spaces to share student work with an audience beyond the classroom, students may take more pride in what they produce and in the fact that they are able to share their product with others. When my students (high school juniors and seniors) create a project for our class, I tell them to think of the work not only as an assignment they will submit for our class, but as something they could show to a future employer or college recruiter as evidence of their skills. Creating for an authentic audience ups the ante for our students.

With the increased availability of technology in the classroom, teachers have far more opportunity to help their students reach an authentic audience than ever before. Teachers can quickly create a class website or learning database using Padlet or Google Sites that allows students to share their work, projects, thoughts, and ideas with each other, and that allows those projects and ideas to be shared with a wider audience. These databases can be resources for future classes, provide samples of assignments that students complete as part of the school curriculum, and offer evidence of learning that students can share with an audience.

By using tools such as Flipgrid and Seesaw, teachers can share student work with other students, students' parents, or school administrators, and provide timely and effective feedback on the projects students create. Flipgrid recently added an augmented reality component to its platform that will allow users to record a video response and use a QR code as a trigger to display the video.

Seesaw provides teachers with another platform for sharing student work. Teachers create classes in Seesaw, add students through a QR code, and easily create assignments that students complete through the platform. These assignments can require students to upload creations ranging from essays or other written documents (saved to cloud-based systems or on their device), share a link to a web-based resource, or provide a photo image, video, or a note that demonstrates their understanding. Teachers can then "like" the student submission (similar to Facebook or other social media posts) and provide immediate feedback on student work. They can also share student creations with family members through Seesaw or share the product with a wider audience through a link or QR code.

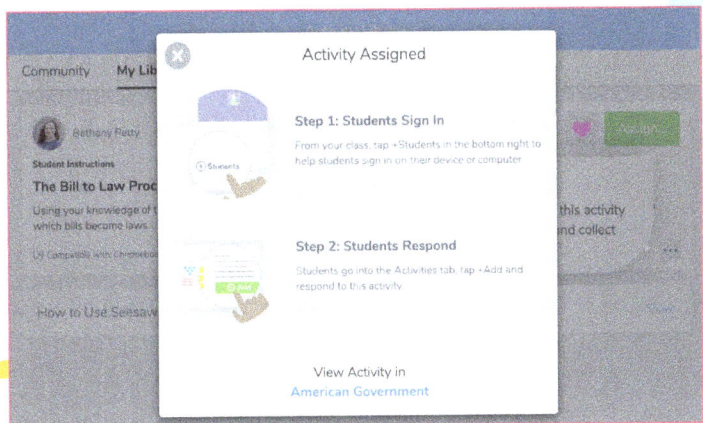

AUDIENCE APPRECIATION

Teachers can also create a "wall of fame" by displaying student creations or QR codes that link to student work. Whether the teacher displays these creations and/or codes inside the classroom, students (or other teachers and administrators) are able to view the work submitted by their classmates. When we know that our work will be shared with a wider audience, we strive to create a better product!

TOOLS FOR SHARING CREATIONS

PADLET

Accessing the tool
- Teachers can create a Padlet wall to share with their students by visiting padlet.com, or by scanning the QR code. When creating a wall, teachers customize the URL, modify the format of the Padlet, and adjust privacy/moderation options to set a password and approve posts before they are viewable by all students.

Student use
- Students can easily share links, videos, images, and files from their device through Padlet. The Padlet wall is quickly accessed through Google Classroom or by link, depending on the teacher's preference.

Sharing student work
- By using a Padlet wall, teachers can collect evidence of student learning and quickly share their students' creations by posting the link to the wall on Classroom, or by creating a QR code to the Padlet link to display in the classroom or throughout the school.

GOOGLE SITES

Accessing the tool
- Students and teachers can access this tool by visiting sites.google.com/new, or by scanning the QR code.

Student use
- Students create their own Google Sites to house their creations or contribute to a class database. To make a collaborative Google Site, teachers create the site and then add students to the site as editors.

Sharing student work
- Students and teachers can share collaborative or individual Google Sites with a link, or by creating a QR code for display that directs an audience to the site.

FLIPGRID 	**Accessing the tool** • Students and teachers can access Flipgrid by visiting flipgrid.com, or by scanning the QR code. **Student use** • Students can access and submit responses to a grid that is created by the teacher. Students create their posts using their smartphone, tablet, or Chromebook/laptop. **Sharing student work** • Teachers can share links to student responses or make the grid viewable to the public.
SEESAW 	**Accessing the tool** • Students and teachers can access Seesaw by visiting seesaw.com, or by scanning the QR code. **Student use** • After their teacher has created class sections through Seesaw, students can access assignments to upload images, video, documents, or drawings that demonstrate learning. **Sharing student work** • Teachers can easily share students' work with their parents using Seesaw, and also communicate directly with parents using the messaging component.

TRY THIS TOMORROW

Create a grid using Flipgrid to encourage students to share their "Top 10" from the chapter, novel, or unit of study for the week. Share the Top 10 grid with an authentic audience by creating a QR code that links to the grid to display outside of the classroom.

SHARING CREATIONS: NOTES

Conclusion: It's Time to Create!

We have amazing opportunities to encourage our students to CREATE every day in our classrooms. By offering them **C**hoice in how they demonstrate learning, we increase the **R**elevance of assignments and activities, which our students demonstrate through **E**vidence of their learning. With frequent **A**ssessment of learning through the products our students create, teachers get a clear picture of the knowledge being understood in our classrooms, the areas in which students need help, and how we can best meet their needs. We can design learning experiences for our students in which they use **T**echnology tools to demonstrate understanding, or that allow them to use other material and resources to show what they have learned. We can encourage our students' **E**ngagement in their learning by allowing them to create products that demonstrate their understanding of content.

A few points to remember:

- Technology should provide students with more options for how they demonstrate learning; it should not be a mandate for our classroom. As we have seen throughout this book, we can encourage our students by offering many high-tech and no-tech options. It's not about the technology; it's how you use it.
- Encourage students to frequently assess their learning by evaluating their creations. Students should be familiar with assignment requirements/rubrics and should be able to evaluate where they are and where they are going in relation to the standards addressed in the rubric.
- Remind students that they should create products for a wider, authentic audience beyond their teacher and peers. Encourage them to create as if they were demonstrating their skills to a future employer or a college recruiter, and watch the quality of work improve.

How will you and your students create in the classroom?

Create

APPENDIX

Tech Tool Index

Anchor (anchor.fm)
Teachers and students create and contribute to podcasts using Anchor. By downloading the app on their smartphone or tablet, students can immediately begin their podcast and share it across podcasting platforms. By sharing their podcast, they are reaching an authentic audience through the intentional use of technology

Book Creator (bookcreator.com)
Students and teachers create and share beautiful e-books using Book Creator. These e-books can be published through Book Creator and shared through link or embed code. Students can create e-books that include text, images, links, maps, and other digital media, and can customize their book with a variety of options.

Canva (canva.com)
Canva provides teachers and students with an easy way to create and share visual aids, including infographics and images. Canva is free to use (premium options are available) for teachers and students, and creations can be shared through links or by downloading to devices.

ClassTools (classtools.net)
This is a great website teachers can use to provide their students with a wide variety of choices for creating products that represent their understanding. Students can create fake text messages, QR code scavenger hunts, Pac-Man–style games, and more for free through ClassTools.

Flipgrid (flipgrid.com)
When using Flipgrid, teachers can create a collaborative space for students to share responses that demonstrate learning. Teachers create grids that are kept private using a password or can be made public to be accessed by a wider audience. Easily share grids by link or by creating a QR code.

Flippity (flippity.net)

A fantastic free tool that all teachers should add to their toolbox, Flippity allows users to create game show–style activities, flashcards, bingo games, "tournament" brackets, timelines, and more to demonstrate learning. Students and teachers can access Flippity templates by visiting the website or by using the add-on available in Google Sheets.

Generate Status (generatestatus.com)

Students use Generate Status to create social media messages that resemble Instagram posts. They then download these posts and share them with their teacher via Google Classroom.

Google Classroom (classroom.google.com)

Since its debut in the fall of 2014, Google Classroom has been helping teachers and students all over the world share creations that demonstrate learning. Teachers use Google Classroom not only to collect student work and provide effective feedback, but also to design a collaborative space for students to share and discuss ideas in a safe environment.

Google Sites (sites.google.com/new)

The "new" version of Google Sites provides students and teachers with a user-friendly platform for creating individual or collaborative websites that can serve as blogs, resource banks, or presentation hubs.

Google Slides (slides.google.com)

As part of the G Suite for Education, Google Slides provides teachers and students with a great and familiar way to demonstrate learning. Throughout *CREATE*, many templates are shared that provide teachers with ready-to-use activities to encourage their students to create e-books, social media graphics, or simulated conversations.

Padlet (padlet.com)

Padlet is an online, collaborative space for students to share ideas, research, and creations. Teachers can create a Padlet wall and customize the format as well as the URL. Padlet walls are easily shared via link, embed code, QR code, or directly to Google Classroom.

Quizizz (quizizz.com)

Quizizz is a game-based assessment platform that allows teachers and students to create and play review activities on a variety of devices. Quizizz offers team or individual modes, as well as a testing option for players, and provides teachers with immediate data to drive instruction. Students can create games through Quizizz to demonstrate learning, review for an assessment, or for a fun closing to a presentation.

QR Code Generator add-on (bit.ly/qr-code-extension)

By using the QR Code Generator add-on in Google Sheets, students can create their own QR code scavenger hunts. These QR codes can be printed and displayed around the classroom or school building, and provide students with a great opportunity to demonstrate what they have learned and quiz their classmates at the same time.

Screencastify (screencastify.com)

Screencastify is a Chrome extension that allows anyone to create a screencast of anything on their computer. Screencastify offers a tab, desktop, or camera recording feature that allows teachers to easily create and share screencasts with their students.

Seesaw (seesaw.com)

Seesaw allows teachers and students to use a collaborative space to share ideas, information, and evidence of learning. Seesaw provides teachers with a great option for sharing student projects with other students, parents, and other stakeholders.

Visme (visme.co)

Students use Visme to create presentations, infographics, and other images to demonstrate learning. These creations can be shared by downloading to a device or sharing through a URL.

Acknowledgments

I am incredibly thankful for the opportunity to share my ideas with the world through this book. While writing it, juggling teaching full-time during the day and part-time in the evening, maintaining my blog, and, most importantly, being a mommy and wife, I kept many verses and words of inspiration displayed around my workspace, including Isaiah 41:10 and Psalm 46:5, to motivate and encourage me.

To say that I am grateful for the support and encouragement my husband has consistently provided me with over the last sixteen years would be a vast understatement. Any ambitious idea I share with him—including writing books; traveling the country to present workshops, keynotes, and seminars; and earning advanced degrees while teaching and parenting—is met with "OK, do it." My daughters, Hanna and Molly, are the biggest blessings I could have ever hoped for and motivate me every day to be the best I can for them. I strive to provide them with a positive example of how they can set and achieve goals in their lives while balancing a career and family. I am also eternally grateful to my parents for their encouragement and support throughout my life, and for being amazing grandparents. My entire family has provided me with unconditional love, which has given me courage to pursue my goals.

I am also eternally grateful for Dave and Shelley Burgess for believing in me and my ideas. I have been fortunate to work in a district with a supportive administration who encourages me to take risks in my classroom to benefit student learning. I have also been blessed with amazing students who have encouraged me to seek out and implement new strategies and ideas to make learning awesome for them.

Finally, I am grateful for YOU! Thank you for reading and seeking out new strategies to use in your classroom to enhance learning. You ROCK! Please follow my blog, Teaching with Technology (usingeducationaltechnology.com), for tips, tricks, strategies, and reflections from my classroom! Be sure to share how you implement the strategies and ideas in this book using #createbook.

About the Author

Bethany Petty is a Christian, mother, wife, full-time high school social studies teacher, adjunct instructor of educational technology, reader, runner, blogger, and coffee junkie. Bethany regularly blogs at Teaching with Technology (http://usingeducationaltechnology.com), where she shares resources, ideas, ed tech tools, tips and tricks, and reflections from her blended/flipped/gamified high school social studies classroom. Bethany's blog was recently listed as one of *EdTech Magazine*'s fifty Must-Read K–12 IT Blogs. She was named a finalist in *EdTech Digest*'s 2017 awards in the School Leader category and was listed as one of the top 100 flipped-learning teachers worldwide. Bethany was recently awarded the VFW National Citizenship Teacher of the Year Award for VFW Post #5741 and for VFW District 8 in Missouri. She was honored with the Outstanding Young Educator award from the Midwest Educational Technology Community (METC) in 2019 and the Secondary Teacher of the Year Award from the Missouri Council for the Social Studies (MCSS) in 2020. She has published posts on Edutopia, Fractus Learning, Sophia Learning, and Whooo's Reading, and she has presented at multiple technology conferences, workshops, and seminars around the country.

Bethany graduated from Southeast Missouri State University in 2008 with her BSEd in Secondary Education with a social studies concentration. She graduated from the University of Missouri–Columbia in 2011 with her Masters in Teaching and Learning. She has earned additional hours in History from Missouri State University.

Bethany is a Google Certified Teacher, Google Certified Trainer, Apple Teacher, Nearpod PioNear, and an EDpuzzle Pioneer. Bethany conducts professional-development sessions in her school district and the surrounding area.

Bethany, her husband Issac, and their daughters, Hanna and Molly, live in Missouri.

Bring Bethany to Your School!

Bethany provides the following workshops and seminars, and can design a customized professional development experience to meet the needs of your staff:

- Using Google Classroom to Enhance Learning (Full-Day Workshop)
- O-M-Google Chrome
- Top Tech Tools for the Classroom
- Using Nearpod to Increase Engagement
- Designing and Utilizing Digital BreakoutEDU
- Increasing Student Engagement through Collaboration
- Motivating Students During Distance Learning
- Creating Your Distance Learning Classroom
- F.I.E.R.C.E. Teaching (Keynote)

What People Are Saying About Bethany's Workshops, Seminars, and Keynotes:

"Outstanding. Best PD I've had in a long time!"

"Excellent seminar - my mind is exploding with so many new ideas and ways to teach the content!"

"Bethany was awesome and provided a lot of great information. Love her energy!"

"This is the best tech workshop I have had. I can see the benefit for my students."

"Thank you! I especially appreciated the real classroom examples."

"Best PD I've ever been to! Bethany was a terrific presenter and provided so much great info!"

"Truly inspiring seminar with great examples that Bethany shared to help us use these tools in our classroom."

Contact Bethany Today!

bethany@bethanypetty.com

@Bethany_Petty

@usingedtech

@bethanypetty_educ8

More from

Since 2012, DBCI has been publishing books that inspire and equip educators to be their best. For more information on our titles or to purchase bulk orders for your school, district, or book study, visit **DaveBurgessconsulting.com/DBCIbooks**.

MORE TECHNOLOGY AND TOOLS

50 Things You Can Do with Google Classroom by Alice Keeler and Libbi Miller

50 Things to Go Further with Google Classroom by Alice Keeler and Libbi Miller

140 Twitter Tips for Educators by Brad Currie, Billy Krakower, and Scott Rocco

Block Breaker by Brian Aspinall

Code Breaker by Brian Aspinall

Control Alt Achieve by Eric Curts

Google Apps for Littles by Christine Pinto and Alice Keeler

Master the Media by Julie Smith

Reality Bytes by Christine Lion-Bailey, Jesse Lubinsky, and Micah Shippee, PhD

Sail the 7 Cs with Microsoft Education by Becky Keene and Kathi Kersznowski

Shake Up Learning by Kasey Bell

Social LEADia by Jennifer Casa-Todd

Stepping up to Google Classroom by Alice Keeler and Kimberly Mattina

Teaching Math with Google Apps by Alice Keeler and Diana Herrington

Teachingland by Amanda Fox and Mary Ellen Weeks

LIKE A PIRATE™ SERIES

Teach Like a PIRATE by Dave Burgess

eXPlore Like a Pirate by Michael Matera

Learn Like a Pirate by Paul Solarz

Play Like a Pirate by Quinn Rollins

Run Like a Pirate by Adam Welcome

Tech Like a PIRATE by Matt Miller

 *Create*

LEAD LIKE A PIRATE™ SERIES

Lead Like a PIRATE by Shelley Burgess and Beth Houf
Balance Like a Pirate by Jessica Cabeen, Jessica Johnson, and Sarah Johnson
Lead beyond Your Title by Nili Bartley
Lead with Appreciation by Amber Teamann and Melinda Miller
Lead with Culture by Jay Billy
Lead with Instructional Rounds by Vicki Wilson
Lead with Literacy by Mandy Ellis
Leadership & School Culture
Culturize by Jimmy Casas
Escaping the School Leader's Dunk Tank by Rebecca Coda and Rick Jetter
From Teacher to Leader by Starr Sackstein
The Innovator's Mindset by George Couros
It's OK to Say "They" by Christy Whittlesey
Kids Deserve It! by Todd Nesloney and Adam Welcome
Live Your Excellence by Jimmy Casas
Let Them Speak by Rebecca Coda and Rick Jetter
The Limitless School by Abe Hege and Adam Dovico
Next-Level Teaching by Jonathan Alsheimer
The Pepper Effect by Sean Gaillard
The Principled Principal by Jeffrey Zoul and Anthony McConnell
Relentless by Hamish Brewer
The Secret Solution by Todd Whitaker, Sam Miller, and Ryan Donlan
Start. Right. Now. by Todd Whitaker, Jeffrey Zoul, and Jimmy Casas
Stop. Right. Now. by Jimmy Casas and Jeffrey Zoul
Teach Your Class Off by CJ Reynolds
They Call Me "Mr. De" by Frank DeAngelis
Unmapped Potential by Julie Hasson and Missy Lennard
Word Shift by Joy Kirr
Your School Rocks by Ryan McLane and Eric Lowe

INSPIRATION, PROFESSIONAL GROWTH, AND PERSONAL DEVELOPMENT

Be REAL by Tara Martin
Be the One for Kids by Ryan Sheehy
The Coach ADVenture by Amy Illingworth
Creatively Productive by Lisa Johnson
Educational Eye Exam by Alicia Ray
The EduNinja Mindset by Jennifer Burdis
Empower Our Girls by Lynmara Colón and Adam Welcome
Finding Lifelines by Andrew Grieve and Andrew Sharos
The Four O'Clock Faculty by Rich Czyz
How Much Water Do We Have? by Pete and Kris Nunweiler
If the Dance Floor is Empty, Change the Song by Dr. Joe Clark
P Is for Pirate by Dave and Shelley Burgess
A Passion for Kindness by Tamara Letter
The Path to Serendipity by Allyson Apsey
Sanctuaries by Dan Tricarico
The SECRET SAUCE by Rich Czyz
Shattering the Perfect Teacher Myth by Aaron Hogan

Stories from Webb by Todd Nesloney

Talk to Me by Kim Bearden

Teach Better by Chad Ostrowski, Tiffany Ott, Rae Hughart, and Jeff Gargas

Teach Me, Teacher by Jacob Chastain

Teach, Play, Learn! by Adam Peterson

TeamMakers by Laura Robb and Evan Robb

Through the Lens of Serendipity by Allyson Apsey

The Zen Teacher by Dan Tricarico

TEACHING METHODS AND MATERIALS

All 4s and 5s by Andrew Sharos

Boredom Busters by Katie Powell

The Classroom Chef by John Stevens and Matt Vaudrey

The Collaborative Classroom by Trevor Muir

Copyrighteous by Diana Gill

Ditch That Homework by Matt Miller and Alice Keeler

Ditch That Textbook by Matt Miller

Don't Ditch That Tech by Matt Miller, Nate Ridgway, and Angelia Ridgway

EDrenaline Rush by John Meehan

Educated by Design by Michael Cohen, The Tech Rabbi

The EduProtocol Field Guide by Marlena Hebern and Jon Corippo

The EduProtocol Field Guide: Book 2 by Marlena Hebern and Jon Corippo

Instant Relevance by Denis Sheeran

LAUNCH by John Spencer and A.J. Juliani

Make Learning MAGICAL by Tisha Richmond

Pure Genius by Don Wettrick

The Revolution by Darren Ellwein and Derek McCoy

Shift This! by Joy Kirr

Skyrocket Your Teacher Coaching by Michael Cary Sonbert

Spark Learning by Ramsey Musallam

Sparks in the Dark by Travis Crowder and Todd Nesloney

Table Talk Math by John Stevens

The Wild Card by Hope and Wade King

The Writing on the Classroom Wall by Steve Wyborney

CHILDREN'S BOOKS

Beyond Us by Aaron Polansky

Cannonball In by Tara Martin

Dolphins in Trees by Aaron Polansky

I Want to Be a Lot by Ashley Savage

The Princes of Serendip by Allyson Apsey

The Wild Card Kids by Hope and Wade King

Zom-Be a Design Thinker by Amanda Fox

www.ingramcontent.com/pod-product-compliance
Lightning Source LLC
Chambersburg PA
CBHW080640170426
43200CB00015B/2906